# NORTHSTAR

## Focus on Listening and Speaking

**Introductory**

Polly Merdinger

Laurie Barton

SERIES EDITORS
Frances Boyd
Carol Numrich

### LONGMAN ON THE WEB

**Longman.com** offers online resources for teachers and students. Access our Companion Websites, our online catalog, and our local offices around the world.

**Longman English Success** offers online courses to give learners flexible study options. Courses cover General English, Business English, and Exam Preparation.

Visit us at **longman.com** and **englishsuccess.com**.

Longman

**NorthStar: Focus on Listening and Speaking, Introductory**

Pearson Education, 10 Bank Street, White Plains, NY 10606

Vice president, instructional design: Allen Ascher
Director of development: Penny Laporte
Project manager: Debbie Sistino
Development editor: Mary Ann Maynard
Vice president, director of design and production: Rhea Banker
Executive managing editor: Linda Moser
Production manager: Liza Pleva
Production coordinator: Melissa Leyva
Production editor: Lynn Contrucci
Director of manufacturing: Patrice Fraccio
Senior manufacturing buyer: Dave Dickey
Cover design: Rhea Banker
Cover illustration: Wassily Kandinsky, "Im Blau," 1925, Detail of central part. © 2002
  Artist Rights Society (ARS), New York/ADAGP, Paris. Photo by Walter Klein/
  Kunstsammlung Nordrhein-Westfalen, Dusseldorf, Germany.
Text design: Delgado Design, Inc.
Text composition: TSI Graphics
Text font: 11/13 Sabon
Photo credits: **p. 1,** © Jose L. Pelaez/The Stock Market; **p. 3,** The Friendship Force; **p. 9,**
  Courtesy Adam Marchuk; **pp. 19, 21,** AP/Wide World Photos; **p. 23,** © Mitchell
  Gerber/CORBIS; **p. 37,** Getty Images, Inc.; **p. 39,** © Bettman/CORBIS; **p. 41,** National
  Museum of Natural History, © 2002 Smithsonian Institution; **p. 49,** British
  Information Services; **p. 57,** Courtesy Dr. Alan Dienstag; **p. 60** top, © Norman
  Schäfer/corbisstockmarket.com; bottom, Photo Researchers, Inc.; **p. 76** Courtesy
  K-K Gregory; **p. 79,** Courtesy Prof. Michael Ray; **p. 87,** Ed Quinn/Corbis Saba; **p. 91,**
  © Bettmann/CORBIS, **p. 92** top left, Getty Images, Inc.; top right and bottom right,
  AP/Wide World Photos; bottom left, © Bettmann/CORBIS; **p. 93,** © Bettmann/
  CORBIS; **p. 94,** Courtesy FDR Library; **pp. 98, 99, 102,** © Bettmann/CORBIS; **p. 124**
  left, Corbis/Stock Market; right, Mr. Nakamura Seiiti—Saitama-shi, Japan; **p. 131,**
  © Franco Vogt/CORBIS; **p. 134** top, © O'Brien Productions/CORBIS; bottom, David
  Young-Wolff/Photoedit; **p. 145** top, © Douglas Kirkland/CORBIS; bottom, Photofest;
  **p. 146,** CORBIS; **p. 155,** © Bettmann/CORBIS
Illustrations: www.Cartoon Stock.com, p. 53; John Dyess, pp. 112, 126, 148, 151; Dusan
  Petricic, pp. 6, 29, 71, 111, 127; Jill Wood, pp. 32, 35, 43, 45, 54, 60, 82, 89
Song credits: See page 184.

**Library of Congress Cataloging-in-Publication Data**

Barton, Laurie.
    NorthStar : focus on listening and speaking, introductory / Laurie Barton, Polly
Merdinger.
      p. cm.
    ISBN 0-201-61980-6
      1. English language—Textbooks for foreign speakers. 2. English language—
Spoken English—Problems, exercises, etc. 3. Listening—Problems, exercises, etc.
I. Title: Focus on listening and speaking, introductory. II. Merdinger, Polly. III. Title.
IV. NorthStar.

PE1128 .B315 2002
428.2'4—dc21

                                                                              2001050533

1 2 3 4 5 6 7 8 9 10—CRK—07 06 05 04 03 02

# CONTENTS

# INTRODUCTION

*NorthStar* is an innovative five-level, integrated skills series for learners of English as a Second or Foreign Language. The series is divided into two strands: listening/speaking and reading/writing. There are five books in each strand, taking students from the Introductory to the Advanced level. The two books at each level explore different aspects of the same contemporary themes, which allows for reinforcement of both vocabulary and grammatical structures. Each strand and each book can also function independently as a skills course built on high-interest thematic content.

*NorthStar* is designed to work alongside Longman's *Focus on Grammar* series, and students are referred directly to *Focus on Grammar* for further practice and detailed grammatical explanations.

*NorthStar* is written for students with academic as well as personal language goals, for those who want to learn English while exploring enjoyable, intellectually challenging themes.

## NORTHSTAR'S PURPOSE

The *NorthStar* series grows out of our experience as teachers and curriculum designers, current research in second-language acquisition and pedagogy, as well as our beliefs about language teaching. It is based on five principles.

**Principle One:** In language learning, making meaning is all-important. The more profoundly students are stimulated intellectually and emotionally by what goes on in class, the more language they will use and retain. One way that classroom teachers can engage students in making meaning is by organizing language study thematically.

We have tried to identify themes that are up-to-date, sophisticated, and varied in tone— some lighter, some more serious—on ideas and issues of wide concern. The forty-nine themes in *NorthStar* provide stimulating topics for the readings and the listening selections, including success stories of young entrepreneuers, the effect of food on mood, the relationship between language and gender, experimental punishments for juvenile offenders, philanthropy, emotional intelligence, privacy in the workplace, and the influence of arts education on brain development.

Each corresponding unit of the integrated skills books explores two distinct topics related to a single theme as the chart below illustrates.

| Theme | Listening/Speaking Topic | Reading/Writing Topic |
|---|---|---|
| Personality | Shyness, a personal and cultural view | Definition of, criteria for, success |

**Principle Two:** Second-language learners, particularly adults, need and want to learn both the form and content of the language. To accomplish this, it is useful to integrate language skills with the study of grammar, vocabulary, and American culture.

In *NorthStar,* we have integrated the skills in two strands: listening/speaking and reading/writing. Further, each thematic unit integrates the study of a grammatical point with related vocabulary and cultural information. When skills are integrated, language use inside of the classroom more closely mimics language use outside of the classroom. This motivates students. At the same time, the focus can shift back and forth from what is said to how it is said to the relationship between the two. Students are apt to use more of their senses, more of themselves. What goes on in the classroom can also appeal to a greater variety of learning styles. Gradually, the integrated-skills approach narrows the gap between the ideas and feelings students want to express in speaking and writing and their present level of English proficiency.

The link between the listening/speaking and reading/writing strands is close enough to allow students to explore the themes and review grammar and reinforce vocabulary, yet it is distinct enough to sustain their interest. Also, language levels and grammar points in *NorthStar* are keyed to Longman's *Focus on Grammar* series.

**Principle Three:** Both teachers and students need to be active learners. Teachers must encourage students to go beyond whatever level they have reached.

With this principle in mind, we have tried to make the exercises creative, active, and varied. Several activities call for considered opinion and critical thinking. Also, the exercises offer students many opportunities for individual reflection, pair- and small-group learning, as well as out-of-class assignments for review and research. An answer key is printed on perforated pages in the back of each book so

the teacher or students can remove it. A Teacher's Manual, which accompanies each book, features ideas and tips for tailoring the material to individual groups of students, planning the lessons, managing the class, and assessing students' progress. The Introductory level of the Teacher's Manual also includes achievement tests.

**Principle Four:** Feedback is essential for language learners and teachers. If students are to become better able to express themselves in English, they need a response to both what they are expressing and how they are expressing it.

*NorthStar*'s exercises offer multiple opportunities for oral and written feedback from fellow students and from the teacher. A number of open-ended opinion and inference exercises invite students to share and discuss their answers. In information gap, fieldwork, and presentation activities, students must present and solicit information and opinions from their peers as well as members of their communities. Throughout these activities, teachers may offer feedback on the form and content of students' language, sometimes on the spot and sometimes via audio/video recordings or notes.

**Principle Five:** The quality of relationships among the students and between the students and teacher is important, particularly in a language class where students are asked to express themselves on issues and ideas.

The information and activities in *NorthStar* promote genuine interaction, acceptance of differences, and authentic communication. By building skills and exploring ideas, the exercises help students participate in discussions and write essays of an increasingly more complex and sophisticated nature.

## DESIGN OF THE UNITS

For clarity and ease of use, the listening/speaking and reading/writing strands follow the same unit outline given below. Each unit contains from 5 to 8 hours of classroom material. Teachers can customize the units by assigning some exercises for homework and/or skipping others. Exercises in Sections 1–4 are essential for comprehension of the topic, while teachers may want to select among the activities in Sections 5–7.

### 1. Approaching the Topic

A warm-up, these activities introduce students to the general context for listening or reading and get them personally connected to the topic. Typically, students might react to a visual image, describe a personal experience, or give an opinion orally or in writing.

### 2. Preparing to Listen/Preparing to Read

In this section, students are introduced to information and language to help them comprehend the specific tape or text they will study. They might read and react to a paragraph framing the topic, prioritize factors, or take a general-knowledge quiz and share information. In the vocabulary section, students work with words and expressions selected to help them with comprehension.

### 3. Listening One/Reading One

This sequence of four exercises guides students to listen or read with understanding and enjoyment by practicing the skills of (a) prediction, (b) comprehension of main ideas, (c) comprehension of details, and (d) inference. In activities of increasing detail and complexity, students learn to grasp and interpret meaning. The sequence culminates in an inference exercise that gets students to listen and read between the lines.

### 4. Listening Two/Reading Two

Here students work with a tape or text that builds on ideas from the first listening/reading. This second tape or text contrasts with the first in viewpoint, genre, and/or tone. Activities ask students to explicitly relate the two pieces, consider consequences, distinguish and express points of view. In these exercises, students can attain a deeper understanding of the topic.

### 5. Reviewing Language

These exercises help students explore, review, and play with language from both of the selections. Using the thematic context, students focus on language: pronunciation, word forms, prefixes and suffixes, word domains, idiomatic expressions, analogies. The listening/speaking strand stresses oral exercises, while the reading/writing strand focuses on written responses.

### 6. Skills for Expression

Here students practice related grammar points across the theme in both topics. The grammar is practiced orally in the listening/speaking strand, and in writing in the reading/writing strand. For additional practice, teachers can turn to Longman's *Focus on Grammar,* to which *NorthStar* is keyed by level and grammar points. In the Style section, students practice functions (listening/speaking) or rhetorical styles (reading/writing) that prepare them to express ideas on a higher level. Within each unit, students are led from controlled to freer practice of productive skills.

### 7. On Your Own

These activities ask students to apply the content, language, grammar, and style they have practiced in the unit. The exercises elicit a higher level of speaking or writing than students were capable of at the start of the unit. Speaking topics include role plays, surveys, presentations, and experiments. Writing topics include paragraphs, letters, summaries, and academic essays.

In Fieldwork, the second part of On Your Own, students go outside of the classroom, using their knowledge and skills to gather data from personal interviews, library research, and telephone or Internet research. They report and reflect on the data in oral or written presentations to the class.

## AN INVITATION

We think of a good textbook as a musical score or a movie script: It tells you the moves and roughly how quickly and in what sequence to make them. But until you and your students bring it to life, a book is silent and static, a mere possibility. We hope that *NorthStar* orients, guides, and interests you as teachers.

It is our hope that the *NorthStar* series stimulates your students' thinking, which in turn stimulates their language learning, and that they will have many opportunities to reflect on the viewpoints of journalists, commentators, researchers, other students, and people in the community. Further, we hope that *NorthStar* guides them to develop their own viewpoint on the many and varied themes encompassed by this series.

We welcome your comments and questions. Please send them to us at the publisher:

Frances Boyd and Carol Numrich, Editors
*NorthStar*
Pearson Education
10 Bank Street
White Plains, NY 10606-1951

# ACKNOWLEDGMENTS

The author and publisher wish to thank the following reviewers for their helpful suggestions on the manuscript:

Elizabeth Ruíz Esparza Barajas, University of Sonora, Sonora, Mexico; Cristina Carillo, San Luis Potosí, Mexico; Mary Peterson de Sanabria, Pontificia Universidad Javeriana, Santafé de Bogotá, Colombia; Sarah Dietrich, Salem State College, Salem, Massachusetts; Michael DiGiacomo, GEOS Language Institute, New York, New York; Nannette Dougherty, Edgemont Junior/Senior High School, Scarsdale, New York; Susan Gillette, Minnesota English Center, Minneapolis, Minnesota; Cristina Narvaez Gocher, Universidad Autómoma de San Luis Potosí, San Luis Potosí, Mexico; Joan Karnes, Lewis Clark State College, Lewiston, Idaho; Kathy Laise, Spokane Work Source, Spokane, Washington; Cathy List, LCP International Institute, Des Moines, Washington; George Murdoch, UAE University, Al Ain, United Arab Emirates; Maria Ordoñez, Universidad de Celaya, Celaya, Mexico; Muge Nure Pehlevan, Yeditepe University, Istanbul, Turkey; Sajida Saeed Tabbara, ELC University of Bahrain, Sakheer, Bahrain.

---

Many people contributed to this book, and I would like to acknowledge all of them. First of all, the *NorthStar* series exists because of the creative vision of Frances Boyd and Carol Numrich. I am very grateful to them for inviting me to contribute to this series.

Frances Boyd edited the original manuscript and offered ideas and support throughout the writing process. I thank her for all of her valuable contributions to the text. Debbie Sistino is the editor that every author dreams of. She guided this book from original manuscript to publication with incredible dedication, professionalism, and good humor. I am especially grateful for the great respect she has for the classroom teacher's point of view. In its last stages, this book benefited tremendously from the editorial contributions of Mary Ann Maynard. Mary Ann worked tirelessly under the pressure of tight deadlines, and always remained in good spirits. Thanks also to Lynn Contrucci for her production expertise, and to the senior editors at Pearson who were involved with this book: Louisa Hellegers, Penny Laporte, and Allen Ascher.

For getting me started on my professional journey, I would like to acknowledge John Fanselow, whose ideas about teaching and learning have guided me. And to my wonderful colleagues at Columbia University's ALP, from whom I have been learning for over 20 years: Thank you for keeping the journey so challenging, so rewarding, and so much fun! You have enriched my life immeasurably. Thanks especially to John Beaumont, for his many valuable contributions to this text, as well as his encouragement.

Finally, and most importantly, for allowing me to share their real stories, I am extremely grateful to Adam Marchuk, Dr. Alan Dienstag, K-K Gregory, Professor Michael Ray, Trent Eisenberg, and Andy Stefanovich. Thanks too to Eli Escobar of WKCR, for educating me about hip hop, to Blanche Wiesen Cook, whose biography of Eleanor Roosevelt inspired me to write about her, and to all the people who assisted me at the F.D.R. Library, and the U.S. Census Bureau.

This book is dedicated to my husband, Ricky, and our daughters, Julia and Nina. I will never have enough words to thank you. I could never have completed this book without your support, patience, and understanding.

PM

I would like to thank the ESL students and faculty at Orange Coast College for everything I have learned from them. I dedicate this book to their continued success.

LB

# "A WORLD OF FRIENDS, A WORLD OF PEACE"

## 1 APPROACHING THE TOPIC

### A. PREDICTING

Look at the picture. Discuss these questions with the class.

1. Are the people friends or family? How do you know?
2. Do you have friends from other countries?
3. Read the title of the unit. What does it mean?

## B. SHARING INFORMATION

**1** *Write your answers to the questions. Then ask a classmate the questions. Write his or her answers.*

| | YOUR ANSWERS | YOUR CLASSMATE'S ANSWERS |
|---|---|---|
| **1.** Have you ever visited another city or country? | | |
| **a.** If *yes*, what cities or countries did you visit? | | |
| **b.** Who did you go with? (alone, with your family, with friends, with a tour group, other) | | |
| **c.** Where did you stay? (in a hotel, with friends, with family, with a host family[1]) | | |
| **2.** What countries do you want to visit? | | |
| **3.** What languages do you speak? | | |
| **4.** What languages do you want to learn? | | |

**2** *Compare your answers with the class.*

---

[1] *a host family:* a family in another country that invites you to live with them for a short time

# 2 PREPARING TO LISTEN

## A. BACKGROUND

A Friendship Force visitor with friends in Vietnam

 **The Friendship Force**

### Friendship Force Member Countries

Australia, Austria, Belarus, Belgium, Belize, Brazil, Bulgaria, Canada, Chile, China (PRC), Colombia, Costa Rica, Cyprus, Czech Republic, Denmark, Egypt, Estonia, France, Georgia, Germany, Ghana, Hungary, India, Indonesia, Ireland, Israel, Italy, Japan, Jordan, Kenya, Kirghizstan, Korea, Latvia, Lithuania, Mexico, Moldova, Netherlands, New Zealand, Norway, Peru, Philippines, Poland, Russia, Singapore, Slovakia, South Africa, Sweden, Taiwan (ROC), Thailand, Turkey, Ukraine, United Kingdom, United States, Uzbekistan, Vietnam

**1** *Read the paragraph. Then do the exercise below.*

"A world of friends is a world of peace." That's the idea of the Friendship Force. The Friendship Force is an international friendship organization. Friendship Force groups travel together to a foreign country. In the new country, each Friendship Force visitor lives with a host family. Friendship Force visitors make about 40,000 new friendships every year. There are Friendship Force clubs in 55 countries all over the world. If you're interested in being a Friendship Force visitor, you can get more information on their website at www.friendship-force.org.

*Read the sentences. Check (✓) yes, no, or I don't know. Then compare your answers.*

|  | Yes | No | I don't know |
|---|---|---|---|
| **a.** Friendship Force visitors want to make new friends. | ❏ | ❏ | ❏ |
| **b.** Friendship Force visitors speak English. | ❏ | ❏ | ❏ |
| **c.** Friendship Force visitors travel in a group. | ❏ | ❏ | ❏ |
| **d.** Friendship Force visitors stay in a hotel. | ❏ | ❏ | ❏ |

**2** *Discuss these questions with the class.*

**1.** Did you know about the Friendship Force?

**2.** Look at the list of countries on page 3. Is there a Friendship Force club in your country?

## B. VOCABULARY FOR COMPREHENSION

*Work with a partner. Read the dialogues. Then circle the best definition of the underlined words.*

**1.** **A:** When did you meet your friend Ruby?
   **B:** <u>Our friendship started</u> in kindergarten, and we are still good friends today.

   **(a.)** We became friends
   **b.** We went to school together

**2.** **A:** <u>Would you like to</u> learn another language?
   **B:** Yes, I'm going to China next year, so I want to learn Chinese.

   **a.** Do you want to
   **b.** Do you enjoy

**3.** **A:** Are you going to <u>join</u> a club at school?
   **B:** Yes, it's a good way to meet new friends.

   **a.** leave
   **b.** be a part of

**4.** **A:** How was the host family you stayed with in England?
   **B:** They were so nice to me. I felt really <u>comfortable</u> in their home.

   **a.** good
   **b.** unhappy

**5.** **A:** You really know a lot about life in Korea.
   **B:** Well, I learned a lot about Korean <u>culture</u> when I lived there.

   **a.** business
   **b.** customs

**6.** **A:** Are you going to get a job after college?
   **B:** No, first I want to <u>travel</u>. I want to see the world!

   **a.** visit different places
   **b.** study different things

7. **A:** How long will you be in Kenya?
   **B:** I don't have much time. I can only <u>spend</u> one week there.

   **a.** stay for
   **b.** pay for

8. **A:** Did you do a lot of <u>sightseeing</u> in New York?
   **B:** Yes, of course! My friends took me to the Statue of Liberty, the Empire State Building, the Metropolitan Museum of Art, and Central Park!

   **a.** walking
   **b.** visiting famous places

9. **A:** What's the <u>cost</u> of a plane ticket from New York to Boston?
   **B:** It's about $130.00.

   **a.** price
   **b.** time

10. **A:** I want to study English at Oxford University next year.
    **B:** You need an <u>application</u>. You have to send it before February 15.

    **a.** a paper to write information about yourself
    **b.** a conversation to give information about yourself

# 3 LISTENING ONE: "Hello. This is the Friendship Force."

## A. INTRODUCING THE TOPIC

*Nina and Rick are talking about the Friendship Force. Listen to the beginning of the conversation. Then answer the questions.*

1. What are you listening to? Check (✓) the answer.

   _____ a telephone call      _____ a radio talk show

2. What will Nina and Rick talk about? Check (✓) your ideas.

   _____ host families      _____ shopping      _____ sightseeing

   _____ hotels      _____ music      _____ groups

   _____ students      _____ children      _____ languages

## B. LISTENING FOR MAIN IDEAS

🎧 **1** *Listen to the conversation between Nina and Rick. Read the sentences. Are they true or false? Write **T** or **F** on the line.*

_____ **1.** Students can join the Friendship Force.

_____ **2.** Everyone is comfortable living with a host family.

_____ **3.** All Friendship Force hosts speak their visitor's language.

_____ **4.** Friendship Force visitors have time to travel.

_____ **5.** Nina wants to join the Friendship Force.

**2** *Go back to Section 3A on page 5. What did Nina and Rick really talk about?*

## C. LISTENING FOR DETAILS

🎧 *Listen again. Circle the best answer to complete each sentence.*

**1.** Friendship Force visitors stay with their host families for _____.

   **a.** two months          **b.** two weeks

**2.** Friendship Force visitors travel around the new country at the _____ of their visit.

   **a.** end          **b.** beginning

3. Rick says _____ to go sightseeing.

    **a.** it's very important       **b.** it's not very important

4. Friendship Force visitors pay _____.

    **a.** their airfare + $100       **b.** their airfare + $1000

5. Nina lives in _____, Ohio.

    **a.** Northfield       **b.** Cleveland

## D. LISTENING BETWEEN THE LINES

**1** *Listen to the excerpts from Listening One. Circle the answer that completes each sentence. Then give a reason for your answer.*

### Excerpt 1

1. Nina thinks that she will feel _____ living with a host family.

    **a.** comfortable       **b.** sad       **c.** uncomfortable

2. Rick thinks that Nina will feel _____ living with a host family.

    **a.** comfortable       **b.** sad       **c.** uncomfortable

### Excerpt 2

Nina is _____ because she speaks only English.

    **a.** worried       **b.** comfortable       **c.** happy

### Excerpt 3

"People, not places" means: You can learn more about a country if you _____.

    **a.** learn the language       **b.** go sightseeing       **c.** meet people

**2** *Discuss these questions with the class.*

1. Did you ever stay with a host family in a foreign country? Where? When? Would you like to stay with a host family? Why or why not?

2. Is it important to speak another language? Do you need to speak the same language to be friends with someone?

3. What are the best ways to learn about another country?

# 4 LISTENING TWO:    The Best Time in My Life

## A. EXPANDING THE TOPIC

🎧 *Listen to Adam Marchuk, a Friendship Force visitor. Then read each sentence. Circle the correct answer to complete each sentence.*

**1.** Adam visited Ukraine when he was a _____ student.

   **a.** high school               **b.** college

**2.** Adam had _____ in Ukraine.

   **a.** a difficult time          **b.** a great time

**3.** Adam's host _____ visited Adam's family last year.

   **a.** brother                   **b.** family

**4.** Adam speaks _____ Ukrainian.

   **a.** a little                     **b.** excellent

**5.** Adam learned a lot from _____ in Ukraine.

   **a.** his host family          **b.** sightseeing

**6.** Now Adam wants to work for _____.

   **a.** world peace           **b.** the Friendship Force

## B. LINKING LISTENINGS ONE AND TWO

Adam (second from right) and Vadim (second from left) with friends in Ukraine

1 *Work with a partner. Read each sentence. Who is speaking? Write* **Nina, Rick, Adam,** *or* **Vadim** *(Adam's host brother). There may be more than one answer for some of the items. Discuss your answers with the class.*

_____  1. I'm going to send my application tomorrow.

_____  2. They were so nice to me.

_____  3. If you want more information, look on our website at www.friendship-force.org.

_____  4. The Friendship Force helped me to decide about my future.

_____  5. I learned more English.

_____  6. Is there any time for sightseeing?

_____  7. People can become good friends, even with no words.

_____  8. His life is very different from our life.

2 *Imagine that Nina is going to call Adam. What questions will Nina ask Adam? What will Adam answer? Write two questions and answers. Then share them with a partner.*

# 5 REVIEWING LANGUAGE

## A. EXPLORING LANGUAGE: Letters of the Alphabet

🎧 **1** *Listen to the names of the letters of the English alphabet. Then practice reading the letter names out loud.*

| | | | |
|---|---|---|---|
| A | /ey/ | N | /ɛn/ |
| B | /biy/ | O | /ow/ |
| C | /siy/ | P | /piy/ |
| D | /diy/ | Q | /kyuw/ |
| E | /iy/ | R | /ɑr/ |
| F | /ɛf/ | S | /ɛs/ |
| G | /dʒiy/ | T | /tiy/ |
| H | /eytʃ/ | U | /yuw/ |
| I | /ay/ | V | /viy/ |
| J | /dʒey/ | W | /dəbəl yuw/ |
| K | /key/ | X | /ɛks/ |
| L | /ɛl/ | Y | /way/ |
| M | /ɛm/ | Z | /ziy/ |

🎧 **2** *It is very important to pronounce the names of the English vowels correctly. Listen to the five vowels and write the letters.*

——  ——  ——  ——  ——

**3** *Talk to three classmates. Ask, "What's your best friend's name? How do you spell that in English?" Write the names on page 11.*

**Example**

STUDENT A:   What's your best friend's name?
STUDENT B:   My best friend's name is Ilhan Ramic.
STUDENT A:   How do you spell that in English?
STUDENT B:   His first name is I-L-H-A-N and his family name is R-A-M-I-C.

Student A writes:   <u>Ilhan Ramic</u>

Student 1: _____

Student 2: _____

Student 3: _____

## B. WORKING WITH WORDS

**1** *Work with a partner.*

> *Student A: Look at this page.*
> *Student B: Look at page 159 in the Student Activities section.*

**A.** *Student A, you are Adam's father. You are talking to Adam on the phone. Ask Adam the questions below. Listen carefully to the answers.*

1. Hi, Adam! How are you?

2. How do you like Ukraine?

3. Are your host parents friendly?

4. Do they speak any English?

**B.** *Continue the conversation. Change roles. Student A, you are now Adam. Listen carefully to your partner's questions. Choose sentence* **a** *or* **b** *to answer the questions. Only one answer makes sense.*

1. **a.** Yes. He just filled out an application for the Friendship Force.
   **b.** Yes. He is learning English.

2. **a.** I think so. He's very interested in American culture.
   **b.** I think so. He's worried about living with a host family.

3. **a.** Yeah. It's important to speak the same language
   **b.** Yeah. It's not important to speak the same language.

4. **a.** Yes, I'm learning a lot about the people and the customs.
   **b.** Yes, I'm learning a lot about world peace.

**2** *Work with a partner. Read the definitions of* noun, adjective, *and* verb *on page 12. Then put each word from the list into the correct group in the chart.*

**Definitions**

A **noun** is a person, place, thing, or idea (*man, country, bus, peace*).

An **adjective** tells something about a noun (a *nice* man, a *good* school, a *big* family).

A **verb** shows action (*speak, learn, live*) or being (*be, become*).

| comfortable | friendship | make | peace | visitors |
| friendly | want | new | speak | |

| NOUNS | ADJECTIVES | VERBS |
| --- | --- | --- |
| | comfortable | |
| | | |

*Now tell your partner three things about the Friendship Force or about Adam. Use words from the chart.*

# 6 SKILLS FOR EXPRESSION

## A. GRAMMAR: Present Tense of *Be*

**1** *Read the excerpts. Follow the instructions.*

RICK:  But you know, the Friendship Force isn't for everyone. Some people aren't comfortable living with a family in a different culture for two weeks.

RICK:  What's your name?
NINA:  It's Nina. N-I-N-A.

1. Underline all the forms of *be*.

2. How many negative forms of *be* can you find? _____

**FOCUS ON GRAMMAR**

See the present of *be* in *Focus on Grammar,* Introductory.

## Present Tense of *Be*

| | |
|---|---|
| **1.** The present tense of *be* has three forms. | |
| *am* | I **am** Nina. |
| *are* | You **are** my friend. |
| | We **are** friends. |
| | They **are** really nice. |
| *is* | He **is** my friend. |
| | She **is** my friend. |
| | It **is** my application. |
| **2.** Contractions are short forms. Use contractions in speaking and in formal writing. | **I'm** Nina. |
| | **You're** my friend. |
| | **We're** friends. |
| | **They're** really nice. |
| | **He's** my friend. |
| | **She's** my friend. |
| | **It's** my application. |
| **3.** To form negative statements with contractions, use a form of *be + n't.* | You **aren't** late. |
| | He **isn't** my brother. |
| | We **aren't** students. |
| | They **aren't** sisters. |
| | The Friendship Force **isn't** for everyone. |
| Do not use negative contractions with *I.* | **I'm not** comfortable. |

**2** *Complete the sentences with the correct form of* be. *Use contractions wherever possible.*

1. We _____ interested in joining the Friendship Force. Can you send us information, please?

2. I love to travel! I _____ afraid to visit foreign countries.

3. The Friendship Force _____ for everyone.

4. Some people _____ comfortable living in another family's home. The Friendship Force is not for them.

5. If you _____ interested in the Friendship Force, call for more information.

**3** *Complete the conversation with the correct form of* be. *Use contractions wherever possible. Then work with a partner. Read the conversation together.*

## Frequently Asked Questions (FAQs) about the Friendship Force

Q:   What kind of people does the Friendship Force look for?

A:   Friendship Force visitors are interested in other cultures. They

_____ afraid of visiting new places.
<br>1.

Q:   Is it necessary to speak another language?

A:   No, it _____! Language _____ a big problem for the
<br>2.    3.

visitors.

Q:   What if we have a problem when we _____ in another country?
<br>4.

A:   Every Friendship Force group has a leader. The leader _____
<br>5.

always nearby. Remember, you _____ alone!
<br>6.

Q:   I _____ interested in the Friendship Force, but I _____
<br>7.    8.

sure when I can go . . .

A:   That _____ a problem. We have many different trips every year.
<br>9.

Just write to us for a schedule.

The Friendship Force
34 Peachtree St. NW (Suite 900)
Atlanta, Georgia 30303 USA

## B. STYLE: Telephone Talk

We say different things when we answer the phone at work and at home.

| At Work | At Home |
|---|---|
| We usually say the name of the company, and sometimes our name:<br>♦ Hello. Friendship Force. Rick (Smith) speaking.<br>♦ Hello. Friendship Force. This is Rick. | We usually answer:<br>♦ Hello? |
| The caller may give his or her name and say:<br>♦ Hello. I'm calling for information about . . .<br>♦ Hi, I'd like some information about . . .<br>♦ I have some questions about . . . | The caller may give his or her name and say:<br>♦ Is Adam there?<br>♦ May I please speak to Adam?<br>♦ May I speak to Adam, please? (NOT: Please may I speak . . . ) |
| We can answer:<br>♦ Sure. What would you like to know?<br>♦ Ok. What are your questions? | We answer:<br>♦ This is Adam.<br>♦ Speaking.<br>♦ Sure, hold on please.<br>♦ He isn't here. Can I take a message? |

**1** *Put the questions and answers for each phone conversation in the correct order.*

**1.** Adam's mother calls him in Ukraine.

_____ Hi. This is Mrs. Marchuk. Is Adam there?

__1__ Hello?

_____ Sure, hold on please.

**2.** Nina calls Rick at the Friendship Force.

_____ Speaking.

_____ Hello, Friendship Force.

_____ Hi, may I please speak to Rick?

**2** _Complete the conversations. Then practice them out loud with a partner. Use the expressions on page 15._

**1.** Vadim calls Adam in the United States.

MRS. MARCHUK: _____?

VADIM:          Hi, may _____ Adam?

MRS. MARCHUK: Sure, hold on a minute.

**2.** Ben calls the American Language Program for information.

MARY: American Language Program. Mary Lee _____.

BEN:  _____. I _____
      your English classes.

MARY: Sure. What would you like to know?

**3.** Nina calls Adam for information.

ADAM: _____?

NINA: Hi, is _____?

ADAM: _____.

NINA: Oh, hi! _____ Nina Rodriguez. Rick
      at the Friendship Force gave me your number.

**3** _Work with a partner. Make up a short telephone conversation. Then role-play it for the class._

> _Student A:_ You work at the Friendship Force.
> _Student B:_ You are interested in the Friendship Force. Call the organization to get information.

# 7 ON YOUR OWN

## A. SPEAKING TOPICS: Talking about Friends

**1** *Do you have a friend in another country? If you don't have a friend in another country, think of a friend in another city. Fill in information about your friend in the list below. Then tell a small group of classmates about your friend.*

**My Friend**

My friend's name is _____.

She/He is from (country) _____.

She/He speaks (language) _____.

She/He is (age) _____ years old.

She/He is a (profession) _____.

OR She/He is studying _____.

She/He is (married/single) _____.

She/He is interested in (hobbies, sports, music, etc.) _____.

**2** *Listen to your classmates talk about their friends. Which of your classmates' friends would you like to know? Why?*

**3** *Discuss this question with the class. Explain your answer.*

Does the Friendship Force really help bring peace to the world?

## B. FIELDWORK

*The Friendship Force works for world peace. Learn about another organization that works for world peace.*

1. Choose an organization. Use the list on page 18 if you need help.
2. Get information about the organization. Use the Internet or a library.
3. Give a report about the organization to a small group of your classmates.

| Organizations for Peace | |
|---|---|
| United States Peace Corps | www.peacecorps.gov |
| Mèdecins sans Frontièrs (Doctors without Borders) | International www.msf.org |
| | United States www.doctorswithoutborders.org |
| Seeds of Peace | www.seedsofpeace.org |
| World Peace Project for Children | www.sadako.org |
| Artists without Borders/ Kids without Borders | www.5abiglobe.ne.jp/~artWB/ |
| Peace through the Arts Camp | www.ptacamps.com |

## Questions to Guide Your Research

1. What is the name of the organization?

2. Who can belong to the organization?

3. What do they do?

4. Where did the organization begin? When?

5. Are you interested in this organization? Why or why not?

## Listening Task

*Listen to your classmates' reports. Write the name of the organization, and ask one more question.*

# DO YOU LIKE RAP MUSIC?

## 1 APPROACHING THE TOPIC

### A. PREDICTING

Look at the picture. Discuss these questions with the class.

1. Who are the people in the picture? What are they wearing?
2. Where are they?
3. What is rap music?

## B. SHARING INFORMATION

🎧 *Read the words and listen to a short part of "Rapper's[1] Delight."*
*Answer the questions. Then share your answers with the class.*

# Rapper's Delight
*Sugarhill Gang (1979)*

I said a hip <u>hop</u>[2]
The hippie to the hippie
The hip hip a hop, and <u>you don't stop,</u> a <u>rock it</u>
To the bang bang <u>boogie,</u> say <u>up jump</u> the boogie,
To <u>the rhythm of the boogie,</u> <u>the beat.</u>
A skiddleebebop, we rock, scooby doo,
And guess what, America, we love you.

1. What are the underlined words about?

   a. love
   b. dance
   c. big-city problems

2. This song has many nonsense words (words with no meaning, not real words), for example, *skiddleebebop*. What are some other examples?

3. Do you like this song? If yes, why?

   a. I like the words.
   b. I like the sound.
   c. It's a good song for dancing.
   d. (Your idea.)

   If no, why not?

   a. The words are nonsense.
   b. There is no melody.[3]
   c. I don't like the sound.
   d. (Your idea.)

4. What kind of music do you like best (classical, rock 'n' roll, jazz, rap, reggae, country, pop)? Who are your favorite musicians?

---

[1] *rapper:* rap musician
[2] *hop:* jump on one foot
[3] *melody:* tune of a song

# 2 PREPARING TO LISTEN

## A. BACKGROUND

Break dancing

**1** *Read the information about rap music.*

In the 1970s, young African-Americans in New York City started something new. They called it "hip-hop." Hip-hop is three things: graffiti art, break dancing, and rap music.

Graffiti artists painted on subway trains and on buildings. Hip-hop DJs[1] played rap music at big dance parties in the streets. Break-dancers danced to the music. The DJs played the music in new ways. Sometimes they played two songs at the same time. And sometimes they repeated one piece of music again and again. Rappers talked with the music.

Rap was different, and young people in the United States liked it a lot. Today you can hear rap music in many languages all over the world.

*Now read the sentences. Write **T** (true) or **F** (false) on the line.*

_____ **1.** Young people started hip-hop in the 1970s.

_____ **2.** Rap is hip-hop dancing.

_____ **3.** Graffiti is hip-hop art.

_____ **4.** Hip-hop started in dance clubs and discos.

_____ **5.** DJs played the music and rappers spoke the words.

_____ **6.** You can hear rap music only in the United States.

---

[1] *DJs:* disc jockeys; people who play recorded music at parties or on the radio

**2** *Discuss these questions with the class.*

1. Have you ever heard rap music before? In what language?

2. Do you like rap music? Why or why not?

## B. VOCABULARY FOR COMPREHENSION

*Read the sentences. Match each underlined word with the correct definition below.*

1. Rap <u>musicians</u> don't play instruments such as drums or guitars. They use electronic machines to make their music.

2. In the first rap songs, the words weren't really important. The songs had <u>rhymes</u> (such as "hip a *hop/*and you don't *stop*"), but a lot of the words had no meaning.

3. The first rap songs were party songs. They had a good <u>rhythm</u> for dancing.

4. In the 1980s, rappers started to write songs about real life. Those rap songs weren't for parties or dancing. They told about the <u>serious</u> problems of people in American cities.

5. A lot of rap songs tell about the problems of <u>poor</u> people. They tell about not having money for food or houses.

6. Some rap songs are about guns and killing. They tell about <u>violence</u> in some American cities.

7. Young people like rap music a lot. It's very <u>popular</u> because it tells about real life.

8. Have you ever heard of Tupac Shakur or Run DMC? They are rappers and they are <u>famous</u> all over the world.

_____ **a.** words with the same ending sound

_____ **b.** action that causes physical pain

_____ **c.** very well known

_____ **d.** liked by many people

_____ **e.** beat or tempo of music

_____ **f.** not funny; important

__*musicians*__ **g.** people who make music

_____ **h.** not having much money

# 3 LISTENING ONE: A Famous Rapper: Tupac Shakur

## A. INTRODUCING THE TOPIC

Tupac Shakur

🎧 *Eli Jones is a radio DJ. He is interviewing King Kool. Listen to the beginning of the interview. Then answer the questions.*

1. Why is Eli Jones interviewing King Kool?

   a. King Kool likes rap music.

   b. King Kool knew Tupac Shakur.

2. Eli Jones and King Kool will talk about Tupac Shakur. What will they discuss? Check (✓) your ideas.

_____ his mother    _____ his CDs    _____ his wife

_____ his friends    _____ his problems    _____ his songs

_____ his money    _____ his future    _____ his childhood

_____ his death

## B. LISTENING FOR MAIN IDEAS

🎧 ❶ *Listen to the interview. Read the sentences. Write T (true) or F (false) on the line.*

_____ 1. Tupac's childhood was difficult.

_____ 2. Tupac's mother had hope for his future.

_____ 3. When Tupac wrote songs, he felt happy.

_____ 4. Tupac wrote songs about his easy life.

_____ 5. Many young people loved Tupac's music.

_____ 6. Tupac wrote rap songs about violence.

_____ 7. Tupac said violence was good.

_____ 8. Tupac died when he was an old man.

❷ *Go back to question 2 above. What did Eli Jones and King Kool really talk about?*

## C. LISTENING FOR DETAILS

**1** *Listen again. Check (✓) the sentences that are true.*

**About Tupac Shakur**

_____ 1. As a child, he was poor.

_____ 2. He never met his mother.

_____ 3. His mother didn't love him.

_____ 4. He was a prince.

_____ 5. He started writing rap songs when he was 13.

_____ 6. He saw violence in his life.

_____ 7. He had problems with the police.

**2** *Listen again. Check (✓) the sentences that are true.*

**About Tupac's music**

_____ 1. His songs were funny.

_____ 2. His songs were serious.

_____ 3. His songs were different.

_____ 4. His music had a good rhythm.

_____ 5. His songs were very popular with young African Americans.

_____ 6. He talked about guns in his songs.

_____ 7. He wrote love songs.

**3** *Discuss these questions with the class.*

1. Have you ever heard Tupac Shakur's music?

2. Do you understand it?

3. Do you like it?

## D. LISTENING BETWEEN THE LINES

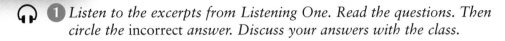

**1** *Listen to the excerpts from Listening One. Read the questions. Then circle the* incorrect *answer. Discuss your answers with the class.*

### Excerpt 1

Why did Tupac feel good when he wrote songs?

    **a.** His songs were happy.
    **b.** He wanted to tell about his life.
    **c.** He liked to write songs.

### Excerpt 2

Why did young African Americans like Tupac?

    **a.** Tupac wrote songs about their lives.
    **b.** They felt Tupac knew about their problems.
    **c.** They wanted to be popular.

### Excerpt 3

How does Caller 2 feel?

    **a.** She doesn't like "gangsta rap."
    **b.** She thinks Tupac's music is bad.
    **c.** She thinks Tupac's music is great.

**2** *Discuss these questions with the class.*

**1.** Did you ever write a song or a poem? Did it make you feel good? Why or why not?

**2.** Is there music that you think is bad? What kind of music is it? Why is it bad?

# 4 LISTENING TWO:    A Rap Song

## A. EXPANDING THE TOPIC

🎧 **1** *Read and listen to part of Tupac Shakur's rap song "Keep Ya[1] Head Up." Then match the line from the song to its meaning below.*

# Keep Ya Head Up

*Tupac Shakur (1993)*

1   Last night my buddy[2] lost his whole family
2   It's gonna take the man in me to conquer this insanity[3]
3   It seems the rain'll never let up[4]
4   I try to keep my head up and still keep from gettin' wet up
5   You know it's funny,
6   When it rains, it pours
7   They got money for wars but can't feed the poor[5]
8   Say there ain't no hope for the youth[6]
9   And the truth is
10  It ain't no hope for the future


___8___  a.  Young people have no hope.

_____  b.  I have to be a strong man to live in this crazy world.

_____  c.  There are so many problems.

_____  d.  My friend's family was killed.

_____  e.  I try to have hope; I try to avoid problems.

_____  f.  The government has money for the military but no
              money to help poor people.

_____  g.  The problems never end.


---

[1] *ya:* your

[2] *buddy:* friend

[3] *conquer this insanity:* stop this craziness

[4] *let up:* stop

[5] *the poor:* poor people

[6] *the youth:* young people

**2** *Discuss these questions with the class.*

1. How is this song different from "Rapper's Delight"? How is it similar?

2. Are there any songs like this in your language? Do people write songs about serious problems?

## B. LINKING LISTENINGS ONE AND TWO

**1** *How are rap songs different from other songs? Work with a partner. Fill in the chart.*

| OTHER MUSIC | RAP MUSIC |
|---|---|
| **1.** The singer sings the words. | The rapper says the words. |
| **2.** The melody is important. | |
| **3.** | The DJ uses electronic machines to make the music. |
| **4.** The songs are about many different things. | |
| **5.** (Your idea) | |

**2** *King Kool said, "Tupac's music will live forever." Do you agree with King Kool? What do you think? Will rap music be popular in the future? Why or why not?*

# REVIEWING LANGUAGE

## A. EXPLORING LANGUAGE: Pronunciation of /æ/

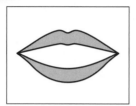

/æ/ is the vowel sound in the word rap /ræp/.

To form /æ/, your mouth is open and your tongue rests on the bottom of your mouth.

🎧 **1** *Listen and repeat these words.*

| | |
|---|---|
| and | that |
| rap | an |
| can | had |
| family | fantastic |
| sad | thanks |

🎧 **2** *Read the paragraph below. Then read it again out loud, softly. Underline every word that has the sound /æ/. Listen to the paragraph and check your answers.*

At first, hip-hop was music, dance, and art. Later, hip-hop began to have its own fashion, or clothing style, too. Rap musicians wore very big pants and T-shirts. On their heads, they wore matching[1] wool hats. Or they wore baseball caps backward. They liked clothes made by famous designers, like Tommy Hilfiger. They liked expensive sports shoes and gold jewelry. Hip-hop fashion became very popular. Soon young people all over the United States had clothes like rappers.

---

[1] *matching:* the same kind and color

**3** *Take turns with a partner. Read the beginning of the sentences out loud. Your partner will complete them with a word from the list. Pay attention to the pronunciation of the words with the /æ/ sound.*

backward      match
caps          rap
fashion       rappers

**1.** Hip-hop music is called _____.

**2.** The musicians who talk in rhyme are called _____.

**3.** On their heads, rappers usually wear _____.

**4.** Another word for clothing style is _____.

**5.** Rappers like to be different. They wear their baseball caps

_____.

**6.** Some rappers like to wear T-shirts and caps that are the same color.

They like to wear T-shirts and caps that _____.

## B. WORKING WITH WORDS

**1** *Read the conversation. Fill in the blanks with words from the list. Then work with a partner. Take turns reading the conversation out loud.*

| | | |
|---|---|---|
| famous | poor | rhythm |
| instruments | popular | serious |
| musician | rhymes | violence |

**An Interview with DJ Eli Jones**

KING KOOL: Eli, who are some important people in rap music history?

ELI: Well, Whodini was the first rap group that used drum machines. Before

Whodini, rap groups used musical _____. Later, many DJs
                                        1.

used drum machines to make rap music. But Whodini started it.

KING KOOL: How about today?

ELI: Well, today, I think Lauryn Hill is a very important rap

_____. She put rap music and soul music together, and she
        2.

started a new kind of music. In her songs, she uses words with the same

ending sounds. These _____ are very interesting.
                              3.

KING KOOL: And what do you think about Will Smith? His music is very

_____ with young people, and he won some Grammies.[1]
        4.

_____

[1] *Grammies* (Grammy Awards): music prizes given in the United States

ELI:     Well, he is very _____. Everyone knows his name because
         5.

he's on TV and in movies. But his rap music is just party music. It has a

good _____ for dancing, but that's it. His songs aren't
         6.

_____. They're just for fun. I like songs that tell about
         7.

real life.

KING KOOL:   But those songs are so sad! Why do young people want to listen to

songs about _____ people? And there is so much
                 8.

_____ in real life. Why do young people want to listen to
         9.

music about guns and fighting?

ELI:     Because it's real! The songs tell what's happening in their cities.

KING KOOL:   Thanks, Eli.

**2** *Discuss these questions with a partner. Use the underlined words in
       your answers.*

1. Do you play a musical instrument? When did you start? What kind
   of music do you like to play?

2. Who is a famous musician in your country? Who is this musician
   popular with (young people, older people, everyone)?

3. Do you have a favorite musician? If yes, does this musician sing
   about serious problems?

# SKILLS FOR EXPRESSION

## A. GRAMMAR: Simple Past of *Be*

**1** *Read the conversations. Then answer the questions.*

ELI:   You knew Tupac. Can you tell us about his life?

KING KOOL:   Well, let's see. His life was too short, and it was difficult. He wasn't a happy child. His family was poor, and he never knew his father.

ELI:   Right. His songs were serious.

KING KOOL:   Yeah. And the words in his songs had really interesting rhymes. They were different from other rap songs.

1. Look at the following words. Find them in the conversations. What verbs come after the words? Write the verbs on the lines.

His life _____was_____        His family _____

it _____        His songs _____

He _____        They _____

2. Find the negative form of *was* in the conversation. Circle it.

**FOCUS ON GRAMMAR**

See the past tense of *be* in *Focus on Grammar,* Introductory.

| The Simple Past of *Be* | |
|---|---|
| **1.** In the simple past tense, the verb *be* has two forms: *was* and *were*. | Tupac Shakur **was** a rap musician. It **was** difficult. His friends **were** rappers too. |
| **2.** To form negative statements with contractions, use *wasn't* or *weren't*. | "Keep Ya Head Up" **wasn't** Tupac's first song. His songs **weren't** funny. |
| **3.** To form a *yes/no* question, use: *was/were* + subject | **Was Tupac** very famous? **Were his songs** popular? |

**2** *Fill in the blanks in the conversation with* was, were, wasn't, *or* weren't. *Then practice the conversation out loud with a partner.*

KING KOOL:  Who is your favorite rap musician?

ELI:  Tupac Shakur. I think he _____ one of the best rappers ever.
1.

But, you know, he died in 1997.

KING KOOL:  Really? How old _____ he?
2.

ELI:  He _____ only 25.
3.

KING KOOL:  How did he die?

ELI:  Well, he _____ always in trouble with people. One night, he
4.

and some friends _____ in a car in Las Vegas, and someone
5.

shot him.

KING KOOL:  How about his friends? _____ they hurt?
6.

ELI:  No, they _____. They _____very lucky.
7.                           8.

KING KOOL:  It's amazing that Tupac's music is so popular today.

ELI:  That's because he _____ so different. He _____ like
9.                                          10.

other rappers. Some people say that he _____ the "Elvis Presley
11.

of hip-hop."

KING KOOL:  But a lot of his songs _____ about guns and killing.
12.

ELI:  Yeah. Those things _____ in Tupac's life, so he wrote about
13.

them. He _____ in trouble with the police many times.
14.

KING KOOL: ＿＿＿＿＿＿＿＿ he ever in jail?
15.

ELI: Yes, he ＿＿＿＿＿＿＿＿ in jail for a few years. That's why some people
16.

didn't like him or his music. They said it ＿＿＿＿＿＿＿＿ good for
17.

children and teenagers to listen to his songs. But Tupac thought music

should be about life.

KING KOOL: Yeah. It's just sad that his life ＿＿＿＿＿＿＿＿ so difficult and so short.
18.

## B. STYLE: Asking for and Giving Definitions and Explanations

When Eli Jones asked King Kool to explain the meaning of "gangsta rap," he said:

*What is "gangsta rap"?*

When King Kool said Tupac's mother called him "The Black Prince," Eli Jones didn't understand. He asked:

*What does that mean?*

### Asking for and Giving Definitions and Explanations

| To ask for a definition or an explanation of a word or expression, we can say: | We can answer: |
|---|---|
| ◆ What **is** that? | ◆ **It's** ＿＿＿＿＿＿＿＿. |
| ◆ What **is** rap? | ◆ **Rap is** hip-hop music. |
| ◆ What **is** a rapper? | ◆ **A rapper is** a rap musician. |
| OR | |
| ◆ What does that mean? | ◆ **It means** ＿＿＿＿＿＿＿＿. |
| ◆ What does "Black Prince" mean? | ◆ **It means** a black leader. |
| ◆ What does "ended in violence" mean? | ◆ **It means** someone killed him. |

**A.** *Work with a partner. Practice asking about words and giving definitions.*

*Student A:* Look at the sentences below.
*Student B:* Look at Student Activity page 159.

*Student A:* Read sentences 1 to 4, one at a time. Student B will ask for definitions. Look at the box. Give the definitions of the words Student B asks about.

**Example**

STUDENT A: Hip-hop artists put graffiti on buildings and trains in New York City.

STUDENT B: What is graffiti?

STUDENT A: Graffiti is hip-hop art. It is writing on buildings and other public places.

1. Hip-hop artists put graffiti on buildings and trains in New York City.

2. I like to watch people break dancing on rap music videos.

3. Tupac Shakur was a famous rapper.

4. In rap songs, the words usually rhyme.

---

**Definitions**

**Graffiti** is hop-hop art.

A **rapper** is a rap musician.

**Rhyme** means the words have the same ending sound.

**Break dancing** is hip-hop dancing.

---

**B.** *Change roles. Listen to Student B's sentences and ask for definitions of the following words:*

1. a DJ

2. nonsense words

3. gangsta rap

4. drum machines

# ON YOUR OWN

## A. SPEAKING TOPICS: Rapping about Rap Music

*Read the things that some people say about rap music. Discuss the questions in small groups.*

1. *"Rap is big-city music."* What does this mean? Rap music is very popular outside big cities, too. Why?

2. *"Rap songs are dangerous."* What does this mean? Do you think it is OK to write songs about violence?

3. *"Tupac lives."* Tupac Shakur died in 1997, but many young people today say, "Tupac lives." What does this mean? Why are young people today so interested in Tupac and his music?

## B. FIELDWORK

*Share a favorite song with your classmates. Follow the steps below.*

**1.** Choose a song you like. Then complete these sentences.

The name of this song is _____.

The singer's/band's/group's name is _____.

The songwriter's name is _____.

It is _____.
                                 What kind of music?

This song is about _____.
                                 Tell the story or idea of the song.

This song is popular now/was popular _____.
                                                      when/where

I like this song/music because it makes me _____.
                                                  feel . . . /remember . . .

**2.** Bring the CD or tape to class. Play it for a small group of your classmates. Tell them about the song and singers, but DON'T READ from your book or paper.

### Listening Task

*Listen to your classmates' presentations. Ask questions about each song.*

# DIAMONDS ARE FOREVER

# 1 APPROACHING THE TOPIC

## A. PREDICTING

Look at the picture. Discuss these questions with the class.

1. What jewels[1] do you see?
2. Do they have any special meaning?
3. Look at the title. What does it mean?

---

[1] *jewel:* valuable stone that you wear as decoration

## B. SHARING INFORMATION

**1** *Work in groups of three. Write the names of the students in your group. Discuss the questions in the chart. Write each student's answers.*

|  | STUDENT 1 (YOU) | STUDENT 2 | STUDENT 3 |
|---|---|---|---|
| **1.** Do you wear jewelry? | | | |
| **2.** What kind of jewelry do you like? Rings? Necklaces? Bracelets? Earrings? | | | |
| **3.** Is jewelry popular in your country? | | | |
| **4.** In your country, do both men and women wear jewelry? | | | |
| **5.** What do women wear? What do men wear? | | | |
| **6.** In your country, do women or men get special jewelry when they get married? | | | |

**2** *Report your answers to the class.*

**Example**

In my group, two people wear jewelry and one person doesn't wear jewelry.

# PREPARING TO LISTEN

## A. BACKGROUND

Queen Elizabeth I, wearing the Crown Jewels

*Read about great moments in diamond history. Then discuss the questions with the class.*

| Great Moments in Diamond History | |
| --- | --- |
| 1200s | English kings and queens begin to collect the Crown Jewels. |
| 1500s | An Italian noblewoman has a diamond wedding ring. The king of France buys jewels from India. |
| 1600s | Rich women in Europe get diamond engagement rings. |
| 1800s | People find diamonds in South Africa. |
| Late 1800s | Cecil Rhodes starts the De Beers Group in South Africa. It soon mines 90 percent of the diamonds in the world. |
| 1940s | De Beers tells Americans "a diamond is forever." Americans buy more diamond engagement rings. |
| 1980s | De Beers tells the Japanese "a diamond is forever." |
| 2002 | 70 percent of Japanese women have diamond engagement rings. |

## Questions

1. When did people first wear diamond engagement rings? Where?

2. Where did people find diamonds in the 1800s?

3. Where did Cecil Rhodes start the De Beers Group?

4. When did Cecil Rhodes start De Beers?

5. De Beers told two countries that "a diamond is forever." What were the two countries?

# B. VOCABULARY FOR COMPREHENSION

*Read the sentences. Then circle the explanation of the underlined words.*

1. Diamonds are very <u>valuable</u>. They cost a lot of money.

   <u>Valuable</u> means _____.

   a. expensive
   b. cheap

2. The Hope Diamond <u>is worth</u> 250 million dollars.

   <u>Worth</u> means _____.

   a. equal to in cost or importance
   b. bigger than

3. Some people like to read books about the history of diamonds. They think this topic is <u>fascinating</u>.

   <u>Fascinating</u> means _____.

   a. very interesting
   b. very boring

4. Diamonds are not all the same size. Some diamonds are very small. Others are <u>huge</u>.

   A <u>huge</u> diamond is _____.

   a. very big
   b. very old

5. A big diamond <u>weighs</u> more than a small diamond. So a big diamond costs more money.

   How much a diamond <u>weighs</u> is _____.

   a. how old it is
   b. how heavy it is

6. An expensive diamond <u>sparkles</u>. When you look at it, you can see light coming from it.

   To <u>sparkle</u> means to _____.

   a. show light
   b. hide light

7. Many people keep expensive jewelry in a safe place. They don't want anyone to <u>steal</u> it.

   To <u>steal</u> means to _____.

   **a.** take something that doesn't belong to you
   **b.** ask to use something

8. Pictures of beautiful diamonds sometimes <u>appear</u> in magazines.

   When something <u>appears,</u> people can _____.

   **a.** buy it
   **b.** see it

9. Some <u>wealthy</u> women wear a lot of diamond jewelry when they go to parties.

   <u>Wealthy</u> means _____.

   **a.** rich
   **b.** poor

# LISTENING ONE:  The Hope Diamond

## A. INTRODUCING THE TOPIC

The Hope Diamond

🎧 *Listen to the beginning of "The Hope Diamond." Read the sentences. Check (✓) Yes, No, or I don't know.*

|  | Yes | No | I don't know |
|---|---|---|---|
| 1. The people are in a museum. | ❑ | ❑ | ❑ |
| 2. The Hope Diamond is valuable. | ❑ | ❑ | ❑ |
| 3. The Hope Diamond is new. | ❑ | ❑ | ❑ |

## B. LISTENING FOR MAIN IDEAS

🎧 *Read the sentences. Listen to "The Hope Diamond." Put the sentences in order from 1 to 3.*

_____ King Louis XIV of France bought the Hope Diamond.

_____ A wealthy woman bought the diamond and had bad luck.

_____ Henry Philip Hope bought the Hope Diamond.

## C. LISTENING FOR DETAILS

🎧 *Listen again. Circle the best answer to complete each sentence.*

1. The Hope Diamond is the most valuable diamond in _____.

   a. the United States
   b. the world

2. The Hope Diamond came from _____.

   a. France
   b. India

3. The Hope Diamond moved to different places, and it got _____.

   a. smaller
   b. bigger

4. The Hope Diamond was missing for a long time because someone
   _____.

   a. lost it
   b. stole it

5. The name of this diamond _____.

   a. is a man's last name
   b. means bad luck

6. The woman who bought the Hope Diamond lost _____.

   a. her family
   b. her money

## D. LISTENING BETWEEN THE LINES

🎧 *Listen to these excerpts from Listening One. Circle the answers. Explain your answers to a partner.*

**Excerpt 1**

Bob _____ the story of the Hope Diamond.

    **a.** knows

    **b.** thinks he knows

**Excerpt 2**

Katelyn _____ the meaning of "Hope" in the name "Hope Diamond."

    **a.** knows

    **b.** doesn't know

**Excerpt 3**

Bob _____ the Hope Diamond brought bad luck to its owner.

    **a.** believes

    **b.** doesn't believe

# 4 LISTENING TWO: Shopping for Diamonds

## A. EXPANDING THE TOPIC

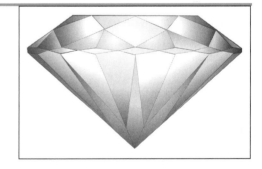

🎧 **1** *Listen to the conversation about the "Four Cs." Then read the sentences on page 44. Write the number of each sentence under the correct "C."*

| Cut | Color | Clarity | Carat |
|-----|-------|---------|-------|
| _____ | _____ | _____ | _____ |

1. Good diamonds usually do not have this.
2. This is what makes a diamond sparkle.
3. This is how much a diamond weighs.
4. Good diamonds are very clear.

**2** *Read the sentences below. Are they true or false? Circle T or F.*

| | | |
|---|---|---|
| 1. Bob wants to marry Katelyn. | T | F |
| 2. Katelyn wants to marry Bob. | T | F |
| 3. Bob and Katelyn know a lot about diamonds. | T | F |
| 4. Bob wants to buy a large diamond. | T | F |

## B. LINKING LISTENINGS ONE AND TWO

*Work in a small group. Read the questions in the chart below. Check (✓) the answers. There may be more than one correct answer. Use information from both listenings. Give reasons for your answers.*

| | COLOR | CUT | CLARITY | CARAT |
|---|-------|-----|---------|-------|
| 1. What was important to King Louis of France when he bought the Hope Diamond? | | | | |
| 2. What makes the Hope Diamond so valuable today? | | | | |

# 5 REVIEWING LANGUAGE

## A. EXPLORING LANGUAGE: Rising Intonation

When we ask *yes/no* questions, we use rising intonation. Our voice gets higher, or rises.

**①** *Listen. Then repeat the questions out loud. Use rising intonation.*

**1.** Are you interested in diamond rings?

**2.** Is this your first diamond?

**3.** Do you have cash?

**②** *Work with a partner. You and your partner will look at similar pictures. How are your pictures the same? How are they different? Ask and answer questions to find out.*

Student A:  Look at the pictures below.
Student B:  Look at Student Activity page 160.
Student A:  Ask your partner *yes/no* questions about his or her pictures. Remember to use rising intonation.

**1.** Do you see a pearl necklace?

**2.** Does it have five pearls?

**3.** Are the pearls big?

**4.** Do you see a diamond ring?

**5.** _____?
    (Your question)

**6.** _____?
    (Your question)

*Then answer your partner's questions about your pictures.*

## B. WORKING WITH WORDS

**1** *Work with a partner. Complete the conversation. Use words from the list. Read the conversation out loud together. Then switch roles.*

| carats | huge | stole | wealthy |
|---|---|---|---|
| fascinating | sparkles | valuable | |

TOUR GUIDE:  The Hope Diamond is worth a lot of money.

TOURIST:  Yes, I know it's very _____.
                                                    1.

TOUR GUIDE:  As you can see, it's also very large.

TOURIST:  Wow! It's _____. How much does the diamond weigh?
                                        2.

TOUR GUIDE:  More than 40 _____.
                                            3.

TOURIST:  This diamond is beautiful.

TOUR GUIDE:  It's beautiful because it _____. Are you interested in
                                                            4.

history?

TOURIST:  Yes, I think history is _____.
                                                    5.

TOUR GUIDE:  The diamond appeared in London in 1812.

TOURIST:  That's right. Someone _____ it from France.
                                                    6.

TOUR GUIDE:  Right. Then a _____ man bought the diamond.
                                            7.

TOURIST:  What was his name?

TOUR GUIDE:  Henry Philip Hope.

TOURIST:  So that's how the diamond got its name!

**2** *Work in a small group. Ask and answer these questions. Use the underlined words in your answers.*

1. Diamonds <u>sparkle</u>. Can you think of other things that sparkle?

2. A diamond is a <u>valuable</u> gift. What other gifts are valuable?

3. The story of the Hope Diamond is <u>fascinating</u>. Can you think of another fascinating story?

# SKILLS FOR EXPRESSION

## A. GRAMMAR: The Simple Present

**1** *Read the sentences. Then answer the questions.*

1. That diamond really sparkles.

2. A valuable diamond weighs a lot.

3. We want to look at some rings.

4. The name doesn't mean "hope" or "bad luck."

5. Small diamonds don't cost as much as large diamonds.

6. You need a lot of money to buy a diamond.

7. Do you have any rings?

**Questions**

a. Which verbs end in -*s*?

b. Which sentences are negative? What are the verbs in these **sentences?**

c. Which sentence is a *yes/no* question?

**FOCUS ON GRAMMAR**

See the simple present in
*Focus on Grammar,*
Introductory.

## The Simple Present

| | |
|---|---|
| **1.** Use the simple present tense for everyday actions or facts. | The diamond **weighs** three carats. Millions of people **visit** the museum every year. |
| **2.** When the subject is *he, she,* or *it,* put an *s* at the end of the regular verbs. Note: *Be* and *have* are irregular. | She **likes** jewelry. It **costs** a lot of money. This diamond **has** a fascinating history. It **is** a valuable diamond. |
| **3.** To form negative statements with contractions, use *doesn't* or *don't*. | He **doesn't like** diamonds. You **don't have** a ring. |
| **4.** For *yes/no* questions, use: Do (or *Does*) + subject + the base form of the verb | **Do you see** the ring? **Does it sparkle?** |
| **5.** For *wh-* questions, use: *Wh-* word + *do* (or *does*) + subject + the base form of the verb | **What do you watch** on Monday nights? **Where do you like** to play golf? **How much does that car cost?** |

**2** *Bob and Katelyn are in London on their honeymoon. They are visiting the Tower of London. Complete the sentences below and on page 49 with the present tense of the verbs.*

TOUR GUIDE: Welcome to the Tower of London and to the Crown Jewels! Are the

Crown Jewels real? How much are they worth? These are the two most

common questions that visitors _____ask_____. The answer to the
<br>1. ask

first question is easy: Of course the jewels are real! And they are old.

You _____ them in old paintings and _____
<br>2. see  3. read

about them in history books. But we

_____ the answer to the
4. know, not

second question. These jewels are

more than gold and diamonds. They

are symbols of 800 years of English

history.

We still _____ the crowns. When a person
5. use

_____ king or queen, he or she _____ one
6. become                                    7. wear

of the crowns. When Parliament _____ every year, the
8. open

Queen _____ the crown. The Imperial State Crown
9. wear

_____ here.
10. be, not

_____ you _____ the huge and
11. see

sparkling Koh-i-Noor Diamond? It _____ 106 carats. The
12. weigh

name means "mountain of light." It _____ like a
13. sparkle

mountain of light! It _____ from India and it belonged to
14. come

Queen Victoria. People think that this diamond will bring bad luck to

any man, so only women _____ it!
15. wear

BOB:    Katelyn, can you believe it? It _____ like the same story
16. sound

again! The Hope Diamond _____ bad luck, too.
17. bring

KATELYN:  I know. Huge diamonds _____ huge stories!
18. have

## B. STYLE: Making Suggestions

---

> *Will you marry me?* is a marriage proposal. It is a special kind of suggestion.
>
> Other suggestions are about something we want to do. We often say *Why don't we . . . , How about . . . ,* and *Let's . . .* when we want to go shopping, go to a movie, or take a walk.
>
> BOB: *Why don't we* go in and look at rings?
> KATELYN: OK. *Let's* look at the diamonds.
>
> BOB: *How about* starting with that one?
> KATELYN: Good idea.

**1** *Read the conversation. Circle the correct suggestions. Then work with a partner. Practice the conversation. Then switch roles.*

1. **A:** I want to buy my mother a pearl necklace.

   **B:** _____

   **a.** How about going to a jewelry store downtown?
   **b.** How about going to Pearl's restaurant?

2. **A:** Good idea. There are a lot of jewelry shops downtown. But I can't drive today. My car isn't working.

   **B:** _____

   **a.** So why don't we take the bus?
   **b.** So why don't we take our time?

3. **A:** OK. Can you go right now?

   **B:** _____

   **a.** Yes. How about going later?
   **b.** No, I can't. Let's go later.

**2** *Complete the conversation. Then practice it out loud with a partner.*

A:  Why don't we go to the movies later?

B:  OK. _____ to the Ritz Theater.

A:  The Ritz is so far away. _____ to the Central Theater?

B:  OK. Good idea.

**3** *Work with a partner. Make up a short conversation like the one in Exercise 2. Then role-play it for the class.*

# 7 ON YOUR OWN

## A. SPEAKING TOPICS: Proverbs or Sayings

**1** *A proverb or saying is a special sentence. It teaches us something about life. Work with a partner. Match the sayings with their meanings below.*

_____ **1.** A good wife is worth more than rubies.[1]

_____ **2.** You speak pearls of wisdom.[2]

_____ **3.** He's a diamond in the rough.[3]

_____ **4.** She's a real gem.

**a.** He is really a good person, but you have to look carefully.

**b.** She is an excellent person.

**c.** A man with a good marriage is rich.

**d.** Your ideas are very good.

**2** *Work in a small group. Think of a popular saying in your language. Tell your group about it.*

---

[1] *ruby:* a red gem

[2] *wisdom:* understanding the right way to live

[3] *in the rough:* inside the rock, before it is cut and polished

**Listening Task**

*Ask each member of your group one question about his or her saying.*

## B. FIELDWORK

**Step 1:**   *Go to a public place such as a park or a shopping center. Look at the different types of jewelry people are wearing. Write what you see.*

---

**Place:** _____

1. What kind of jewelry do you see on men (for example, rings, necklaces, bracelets, earrings)?

2. What kind of jewelry do you see on women?

3. Who is wearing the most jewelry (children, teenagers, young adults, middle-aged adults, older adults)?

---

**Step 2:**   *Work in a small group. Compare your answers to the questions in step 1.*

**Step 3:**   *Tell the class the most interesting information from step 1 and step 2.*

**Listening Task**

*Listen to your classmates. What kind of jewelry do most women wear? What kind of jewelry do most men wear? Who wears the most jewelry?*

# MEMORIES: LOST AND FOUND

From www.CartoonStock.com.

# 1 APPROACHING THE TOPIC

## A. PREDICTING

Look at the cartoon. Discuss these questions with the class.

1. Where are the people?
2. What did the man forget? What is the title of the book?
3. Do you know anyone who often forgets things?

## B. SHARING INFORMATION

**1** *Look at the picture below for one minute. Then close your book and write down as many things as you can remember about the picture.*

**2** *Compare your list with a partner's. Then look at the picture again and discuss these questions:*

**1.** How many things did you remember?

**2.** Who remembered more things?

**3.** Did you remember any of the same things? Any different things?

**3** *Discuss these questions with the class.*

**1.** Who remembered the most things from the picture?

**2.** Why did you remember some things but not others?

**3.** Do you have any special ways to remember things?

**4.** Are birthdays and telephone numbers easy for you to remember? What things are usually easy to remember? What things are difficult?

# 2 PREPARING TO LISTEN

## A. BACKGROUND

**1** *Read the information about Alzheimer's disease.*

(1) Four million older Americans have Alzheimer's disease. (2) People with Alzheimer's disease cannot remember things. (3) At first, they can't remember words and names. (4) Then they can't remember what they are doing. (5) Sometimes they don't know where they are. (6) They can't remember how to do everyday things. (7) Later they don't remember their friends or family members. (8) Many people with Alzheimer's disease lose their friends.

(9) Doctors have no cure[1] for Alzheimer's, but they are trying to help people with this disease. (10) One way is with support[2] groups. (11) In support groups, people with Alzheimer's meet together and talk about their feelings.

**2** *Read the things some people with Alzheimer's disease said in their support group. Some of the sentences in the reading have the same idea as the sentences below. Write the number of the sentence from the reading on the line. Check your answers with a partner.*

___6___ **a.** "I can't drive a car anymore because I can't remember how."

—Sarah, 75 years old

_____ **b.** "I can't remember how to get places. Sometimes I don't know where I'm going."

—Elsa, 74 years old

_____ **c.** "My friends don't visit me anymore. When people know you have Alzheimer's, you never see them again."

—Sam, 68 years old

_____ **d.** "I can't enjoy a book or a movie anymore, because when I get to the middle, I can't remember the beginning."

—Rhoda, 60 years old

---

[1] *cure:* drug or medicine to bring health

[2] *support:* help

## B. VOCABULARY FOR COMPREHENSION

*Read the sentences. Then circle the definition of the underlined words.*

1. When my husband got sick, my mother and my sisters helped me to take care of him. My <u>relatives</u> were so helpful.

   <u>Relatives</u> are _____.

   **a.** family
   **b.** friends

2. Our book club meets once a month. We talk about interesting books. The <u>members</u> are very nice people.

   <u>Members</u> are _____.

   **a.** people who belong to a group
   **b.** people who remember many things

3. My grandfather is getting older. He sometimes <u>forgets</u> things. For example, when he tells me a story, he sometimes forgets words.

   <u>Forgets</u> means _____.

   **a.** doesn't remember
   **b.** writes down

4. Doctors help sick people to become healthy. Psychologists help people to <u>feel better about themselves</u>.

   When you <u>feel better about yourself</u>, you _____.

   **a.** are happier
   **b.** are nervous

5. Rhoda and Sarah are very good friends. They always tell <u>each other</u> about their feelings and problems.

   When they tell <u>each other</u>, _____.

   **a.** Rhoda and Sarah tell all the people they know
   **b.** Rhoda tells Sarah and Sarah tells Rhoda

6. I don't want to <u>lose</u> my old friends when I go to the United States. I'm going to e-mail or call them every day.

   <u>Lose</u> means _____.

   **a.** keep
   **b.** not keep

7. When June's family moved to a new city, she didn't know anyone at her new school. She felt very <u>lonely</u>.

She <u>felt lonely</u> means she felt _____.

  **a.** unhappy because she had no friends
  **b.** afraid because she was alone

8. My grandmother came to the United States 40 years ago, but she remembers many things about her native country. She often tells us about her happy childhood <u>memories</u>.

<u>Memories</u> are _____.

  **a.** things that people remember
  **b.** problems that people have

# LISTENING ONE:    "I Remember"

## A. INTRODUCING THE TOPIC

Dr. Alan Dienstag (center)

Jane Oliver works at the Alzheimer's Association. Every month, families of people with Alzheimer's have a meeting there. They want to learn how to help their relatives.

*Listen. Jane Oliver is introducing Dr. Alan Dienstag. Dr. Dienstag works with people who have Alzheimer's. Do you think Dr. Dienstag will talk about the things below? Check (✓) Yes or No.*

|  | Yes | No |  | Yes | No |
|---|---|---|---|---|---|
| 1. New medicines | ❏ | ❏ | 6. Feeling lonely | ❏ | ❏ |
| 2. Listening to music | ❏ | ❏ | 7. Childhood memories | ❏ | ❏ |
| 3. Writing stories | ❏ | ❏ | 8. Remembering names | ❏ | ❏ |
| 4. Making friends | ❏ | ❏ | 9. Teenagers' problems | ❏ | ❏ |
| 5. Different cultures | ❏ | ❏ | 10. Support groups | ❏ | ❏ |

## B. LISTENING FOR MAIN IDEAS

🎧 **①** *Listen to Dr. Dienstag. Write* **T** *if the sentences are true. Write* **F** *if the sentences are false.*

_____ 1. The members of the writers' group write about their memories.

_____ 2. The members listen to each other's stories.

_____ 3. People with Alzheimer's forget many things.

_____ 4. The group members meet to study Alzheimer's disease together.

_____ 5. The group members become good friends.

_____ 6. Alzheimer's disease is not a terrible disease.

_____ 7. The group members are happy to meet with each other.

**②** *Look back at page 57. What things did Dr. Dienstag talk about?*

## C. LISTENING FOR DETAILS

🎧 *Listen again. Circle the best answer.*

1. How often does the writers' group meet?

   a. once a week
   b. twice a week
   c. every month

2. What do people with Alzheimer's disease usually remember?

   a. stories
   b. the past
   c. the present

3. How do the group members help each other?

   a. They find old friends.
   b. They find ideas.
   c. They find words.

4. Why do many people with Alzheimer's feel lonely?

   a. They lose their friends.
   b. They are old.
   c. They live alone.

5. What are the first words of every story?

    **a.** "I don't remember."
    **b.** "I'm a member."
    **c.** "I remember."

6. Why are the group members happy to meet together?

    **a.** They need to finish their stories.
    **b.** They have a good time together.
    **c.** They want to live together.

## D. LISTENING BETWEEN THE LINES

 ① *Listen to the excerpts from Listening One. Circle the best way to complete the sentences.*

### Excerpt 1

The speaker doesn't think that _____.

    **a.** his father has Alzheimer's disease
    **b.** writing can help his father

### Excerpt 2

Dr. Dienstag wants his group members to _____.

    **a.** remember everything from their past
    **b.** feel good about themselves

### Excerpt 3

The woman thinks that the writers' group can make people _____.

    **a.** less lonely
    **b.** wonderful writers

② *Discuss these questions with the class.*

1. What do you think about the writers' group? Is it a good idea? Why or why not?

2. What do you think about the family meetings at the Alzheimer's Association? How do they help the families?

3. Do you know anyone who has Alzheimer's disease? Tell about that person.

# 4 LISTENING TWO: Elsa's Story

## A. EXPANDING THE TOPIC

🎧 **1** *Listen to Elsa, a member of the writers' group. She is reading her story to Dr. Dienstag and the other members of the group. Write **T** if the sentence is true. Write **F** if the sentence is false.*

_____ **1.** Elsa's story is about a childhood memory.

_____ **2.** In her story, the clouds in the sky looked like waves.

_____ **3.** Elsa forgot the special name for that kind of sky.

_____ **4.** A mackerel fish was in the sky.

_____ **5.** A group member helped Elsa to find the right words for her story.

_____ **6.** Elsa's story is finished.

Mackerel fish

**2** *Discuss these questions with the class.*

1. How did Sarah feel when she remembered the phrase "mackerel sky"? Excited? Sad?

2. How did Elsa feel when Sarah helped her? Angry? Sad? Happy?

3. What do you think about the writers' group now? Did your opinion change? Why or why not?

## B. LINKING LISTENINGS ONE AND TWO

**1** *Think about Dr. Dienstag's group and Elsa's story. Work with a partner and make two lists. Think about all the things that people with Alzheimer's disease can't remember and can't do anymore. What things have they "lost"? Think about the members of the Alzheimer's writers' group. What have they "found"?*

| **People with Alzheimer's disease have lost:** | **People in the writers' group have found:** |
|---|---|
| their memories | new friends |
| _____ | _____ |
| _____ | _____ |
| _____ | _____ |

*Now compare your lists with the class.*

**2** *Read the statements below. Do you agree or disagree? Check (✓) your opinion. Then discuss your answers with the class.*

|  | I agree | I disagree |
|---|---|---|
| 1. All older people need groups, not just people with Alzheimer's disease. | ❏ | ❏ |
| 2. Thinking about the past is not good for elderly people. | ❏ | ❏ |

## REVIEWING LANGUAGE

### A. EXPLORING LANGUAGE: Pronunciation of /ey/ and /ɛ/

/ey/ is the vowel sound in the word *way* /wey/. It is called a "tense" sound because you tense (or stretch) your lips when you make this sound (like a smile). Your tongue is in the center of your mouth.

/ɛ/ is the vowel sound in the word *when* /wɛn/. It is called a "lax" or "relaxed" sound because you do not stretch your lips. Your lips feel relaxed. Your tongue is a little lower and farther back than for /ey/. Your jaw is a little more open.

🎧 **1** *Listen to and repeat these words.*

| /ey/ | /ɛ/ |
|------|------|
| may | yes |
| name | forget |
| waves | remember |
| they | help |
| always | many |

🎧 **2** *Listen to these words. Is the vowel sound /ey/ or /ɛ/? Circle the answer.*

1. welcome /ey/ or /ɛ/     5. daytime /ey/ or /ɛ/

2. member /ey/ or /ɛ/     6. together /ey/ or /ɛ/

3. same /ey/ or /ɛ/     7. make /ey/ or /ɛ/

4. better /ey/ or /ɛ/     8. friends /ey/ or /ɛ/

🎧 **3** *Listen to and silently read Jane Oliver's and Dr. Dienstag's conversation below and on page 63. Then work with a partner. Write /ey/ or /ɛ/ above the bold letters. Check your answers in the Answer Key.*

JANE OLIVER:    Dr. Dienstag, I have a question, too. How did you get the idea for an Alzheimer's writers' group?

DR. DIENSTAG:    1.  /ɛ/ /ey/
Well, I have to say, it really wasn't my idea!

2.  / /  / /  / /
The idea came from a famous writer named Don DeLillo.

3. His mother-in-law had Alzheimer's, and I met her.

4. She wanted to remember things.

5. But she was forgetting more and more every day.

6. Don DeLillo was looking for a way to help his mother-in-law.

7. One day, he told me his idea about a writers' group.

8. I thought it was a great idea.

9. So we decided to work together.

**4** *Work with a partner. Take turns reading Dr. Dienstag's sentences out loud. Listen to your partner's pronunciation and correct any mistakes. Then listen to the conversation again to check your pronunciation.*

## B. WORKING WITH WORDS

**1** *Work with a partner.*

> *Student A: Look at this page.*
> *Student B: Look at Student Activity page 161.*
> *Student A: Read the sentence. Listen to your partner's response. Does it make sense? If it doesn't make sense, tell your partner, "I don't think that's right."*

1. My aunt has Alzheimer's disease.

2. The Alzheimer's Association has special meetings for the families of people with Alzheimer's.

3. Sometimes I can't remember a word or a person's name.

4. Some people with Alzheimer's feel very sad about their lives.

*Change roles. Listen to your partner's sentences. Choose the correct response.*

e. I know. She was so sad to lose her job. She really loved it.

f. That's right. The writers all help each other.

g. Yes! I have a clear memory of my third birthday! I remember everything from that day.

h. Right. And then they don't feel so lonely.

**2** *Look at the pairs of words below. Think about their meanings. Are they the same (S) or different (D)? Circle S or D.*

| | | | |
|---|---|---|---|
| **1.** disease | illness | S | D |
| **2.** talk about | discuss | S | D |
| **3.** lose | keep | S | D |
| **4.** forget | remember | S | D |
| **5.** tell about | explain | S | D |
| **6.** feel worse | feel better | S | D |
| **7.** support | help | S | D |

# 6 SKILLS FOR EXPRESSION

## A. GRAMMAR: Subject and Object Pronouns

**1** *Read the following statements. Look at the underlined words. Then answer the questions.*

1. "I can't drive a car anymore. Someone has to take <u>me</u> everywhere."

—Sarah

2. "Rhoda was a very successful fashion designer. But now, <u>she</u> doesn't know what clothes to wear. I have to help <u>her</u> get dressed."

—Herb (Rhoda's husband)

**Questions**

**a.** Which underlined words are subjects?

_____

_____

**b.** Which underlined words are objects?

_____

_____

**FOCUS ON GRAMMAR**

See subject and object pronouns in *Focus on Grammar,* Introductory.

| **Subject and Object Pronouns** | |
|---|---|
| Pronouns take the place of nouns. We use pronouns when we do not want to repeat the same noun many times in a sentence or a conversation. | |
| **1.** *Subject pronouns* take the place of the subject in a sentence.<br><br>Subject pronouns include *I, you, he, she, it, we,* and *they.* | **Sam** had many friends.<br>**He** had many friends. |
| **2.** *Object pronouns* take the place of an object.<br><br>Object pronouns include *me, you, him, her, it, us,* and *them.* | Some friends stopped visiting **Sam**.<br>Some friends stopped visiting **him**. |
| **3.** Object pronouns can follow *prepositions.*<br><br>Prepositions that can be followed by an object pronoun include *to, for,* and *from.* | Sam never spoke to ***those friends*** again.<br>Sam never spoke to **them** again. |

**2** *Sarah's daughter, Jennifer, tells her about the writers' group. Read the conversation aloud with a partner. Write the correct pronouns.*

JENNIFER: Mom, the Alzheimer's Association has a new group. _____'s a

  1.

  writers' group. Are _____ interested?

  2.

SARAH: Jennifer, I have Alzheimer's! How can _____ join a writers' group?

  3.

JENNIFER: I'll tell you. A psychologist named Alan Dienstag started the group.

  _____ says that the group members help each other. And

  4.

  _____ feel better about themselves, too.

  5.

SARAH: Really? Why?

JENNIFER:  Because they make new friends. And that helps _____ a lot.
6.

SARAH:  But, Jennifer, people with Alzheimer's can't write well. We're losing our

memories. No one can help _____!
7.

JENNIFER:  Well, Dr. Dienstag showed me a video of the group and _____
8.

thought it was really interesting. One woman read a story and

everybody helped _____ with the words. _____
9.                                    10.

looked so happy!

SARAH:  Well, OK, maybe _____ will go.
11.

JENNIFER:  That's great, Mom. I think you'll like _____. Can I call Dr.
12.

Dienstag?

SARAH:  OK. I'll talk to _____ tomorrow.
13.

## B. STYLE: Expressing Interest in a Conversation

When Dr. Dienstag talks to the family group, some of the relatives use
expressions to show him that they are interested in his ideas.

DR. DIENSTAG:  It's difficult for them to explain their ideas. But when they meet in a
group, they can help each other.

RELATIVE 1:  (*still unsure*) Really?

DR. DIENSTAG:  Yes, it's amazing. Together, they find the right words to explain their
ideas. And then they all feel better about themselves.

RELATIVE 2:  (*excited*) I think that's wonderful! And it's a nice way to make new
friends, too.

DR. DIENSTAG:  Yes, and that's very important.

DR. DIENSTAG:    Well, every week, they write about a different memory. But they always begin with the same two words: "I remember."

RELATIVE 3:    That's interesting. We usually think about the things they *don't* remember.

DR. DIENSTAG:    That's true.

Here are some useful *expressions of interest*.

When you hear any new information:
- Really . . .
- Uh-huh . . .
- Oh, really?

When you hear interesting or exciting information:
- That's (so) interesting!
- That's great!
- That's wonderful!
- That's amazing!

*Work with a partner to complete the dialogue below and on page 68. Use expressions of interest from the box above. Read the dialogue with your partner. Then change roles.*

**A:**    I have some good news. I stopped smoking!

**B:**    _____! Congratulations! How did you do it?

**A:**    I joined a group called Smokenders, and I go to their meetings every week. The meetings really help a lot.

**B:**    _____. What do you do at the meetings?

**A:**    Well, we learn different ways to stop smoking. And the members talk about their feelings. It's like a support group. I'm learning a lot about myself!

**B:**    _____. What did you learn?

**A:**    Well, I realized that I smoked a lot when I was nervous. Smoking made me feel more comfortable.

**B:** _____. Did you learn anything else?

**A:** Yeah. I learned that exercise is a much better way to relax, so now I run two miles every day. I feel better about myself, and now I don't even *want* a cigarette.

**B:** Two miles a day! _____! Smokenders sounds like a great organization.

**A:** Yeah, it really is!

# ON YOUR OWN

## A. SPEAKING TOPICS: With a Group or Alone?

**1** *What kinds of things do you like to do* with other people? *What kinds of things do you prefer to do* alone? *Check (✓) your answers in the list below.*

|  | With other people | Alone |
|---|---|---|
| Write | ❏ | ❏ |
| Listen to music | ❏ | ❏ |
| Exercise in a gym | ❏ | ❏ |
| Walk, jog, or run | ❏ | ❏ |
| Travel, sightsee | ❏ | ❏ |
| Eat | ❏ | ❏ |
| Do homework | ❏ | ❏ |
| Study for a test | ❏ | ❏ |
| Go to the movies | ❏ | ❏ |
| Work on a hobby (draw, paint, take photos, build things, etc.) | ❏ | ❏ |
| Go shopping | ❏ | ❏ |
| Other things? (your own ideas) | ❏ | ❏ |

**2** *Now compare your answers with a partner's. Give reasons for your answers. Remember to use expressions of interest when your partner is speaking.*

**3** *Work in a group. Discuss these questions.*

1. Were you ever a member of a group or club?

2. What kind of group was it? (study group, sports club, hobby club, chorus, drama group)

3. Did you make any good friends in that group? Why or why not?

**4** *Take turns. Tell the class one interesting thing you learned about another student.*

### Listening Task

*Listen to your classmates tell interesting things about other students. Respond with appropriate expressions of interest. Which of your classmates was in the most interesting group or club?*

### Example

STUDENT A:  Linda is a member of a skydiving club.
STUDENT B:  That's great!

## B. FIELDWORK

**1** *Interview an elderly or middle-aged person that you know (a family member, friend, neighbor, or teacher). Begin like this:*

May I ask you some questions about your life?

Do you mind if I ask you some questions about your life?

*Ask the interview questions on page 70. Take notes.*

**Interview questions**

*About the past*

1. What is your earliest memory?
2. Where did you grow up?
3. Where did you go to school?
4. Did you have a best friend in school? What did you like about this person?
5. What was your first job? Did you like it?
6. What is your happiest memory?

*About now*

7. Do you work? What do you (OR did you) do?
8. Do you have any hobbies?
9. Who is your best friend now?
10. Are you a member of any groups? What kind?
11. (Your questions)

2 *Tell the class one interesting thing about the person you interviewed. Use your notes.*

**Listening Task**

*Listen to your classmates' reports. Take turns using expressions of interest when your classmates are speaking.*

# THINKING YOUNG: CREATIVITY IN BUSINESS

Picture 1

Picture 2

# 1 APPROACHING THE TOPIC

## A. PREDICTING

Look at the pictures. Discuss these questions with the class.

1. What are the co-workers doing in Picture 1? How do they feel?
2. What are the same co-workers doing in Picture 2? How do they feel?
3. Look at the title of the unit. What is this unit about?

## B. SHARING INFORMATION

Creative people have new and unusual ideas. Sometimes they create or make new things. Children are usually creative when they play. They have many new ideas.

**1** *Read the questions and circle your answers.*

1. When you were a child, what creative thing(s) did you do?

    a. I created a new game or toy.
    b. I created a piece of art (painting, sculpture).
    c. I wrote a song or played a musical instrument.
    d. I wrote a story or poem.
    e. I solved a problem in an unusual way.
    f. (something else?) _____

2. When you were creative, how did you feel? Choose all the words that explain your feelings. Use your dictionary for help.

    a. proud
    b. excited
    c. happy
    d. nervous
    e. (another feeling?) _____

**2** *Interview three students about their creative experiences. Write their answers in the chart.*

| | WHAT DID YOU DO? | HOW DID YOU FEEL? |
|---|---|---|
| Student 1 | | |
| Student 2 | | |
| Student 3 | | |

*Now share some of your answers with the class.*

# PREPARING TO LISTEN

## A. BACKGROUND

**1** *Read the information from* Fast Company, *a business magazine.*

Creative workers help companies to succeed. So, many companies (for example, American Express, Disney, Microsoft, Kinko's) spend billions of dollars a year on creativity training. They have creativity classes for their employees. In these creativity classes, employees learn how to "think young." They relax and play, like children. After creativity training, employees usually have new ideas for their companies.

What do people do in creativity training? At Play, an advertising agency in Virginia, employees do exciting sports together, such as white-water rafting or rock climbing. And at Stanford University Graduate School of Business in California, students learn to meditate.[1] These are two ways to help businesspeople to relax and get new ideas. Businesspeople are learning that it's good to think young—it's good for business!

**2** *Complete these sentences with a partner. Then compare your answers with the class.*

1. American Express and Disney think that creative employees are
   _____.

   a. good for business
   b. very young

2. Creativity trainers think that children are more _____ than adults.

   a. intelligent
   b. creative

3. Doing sports and meditating can help employees to _____.

   a. get a better job
   b. be more creative

---

[1] *meditate:* sit quietly in one place to feel calm and think

**3** *Discuss these questions with the class.*

Are children more creative than adults?

Why do you think so?

## B. VOCABULARY FOR COMPREHENSION

**1** *Work with a partner. Read the conversations. Circle the sentence that has the same meaning as the underlined sentence.*

1. A: How's your brother's new computer business?
   B: <u>It's very *successful*</u>! He's making a lot of money!
   a. He's selling a lot of computers.
   b. He likes computers a lot.

2. A: Who is that woman?
   B: That's Elaine! <u>She's the *owner* of Elaine's, the famous New York restaurant.</u>
   a. She works in Elaine's restaurant.
   b. Elaine's is her restaurant.

3. A: It's so cold here! I'm freezing!
   B: I have an idea. <u>Let's *move around* to stay warm.</u> We can jump up and down.
   a. Let's keep our arms and legs in the same place.
   b. Let's change the position of our arms and legs.

4. A: Can I wear this winter coat for skiing?
   B: No, it's too long. You won't be comfortable. <u>It's better to wear a *jacket*.</u>
   a. You should wear a warm coat.
   b. You should wear a short coat.

5. A: Do you like this winter hat?
   B: Yeah! <u>What kind of *material* is it?</u> It's very warm.
   a. What is it made of?
   b. What style is it?

6. A: You can't wear those jeans to school! <u>They have *holes* in them!</u>
   B: That's the style, Mom. I really like these jeans!
   a. They're not clean.
   b. They have openings.

7. **A:** <u>Please tell us about your work *experience.*</u>
   **B:** Well, I was an assistant manager at Sony for 2 years, and then I started to work at Dell as a manager.
   **a.** Tell us about your past jobs.
   **b.** Tell us about your education.

8. **A:** <u>Starting a new business is very *exciting*</u>!
   **B:** Yes, but it's also a lot of hard work.
   **a.** Starting a new business costs a lot of money.
   **b.** Starting a new business is a lot of fun.

9. **A:** What's the matter?
   **B:** I have a problem at work. I'm not sure what to do. <u>Can you give me some *advice*?</u>
   **a.** Can you answer my questions?
   **b.** Can you help me do my work?

10. **A:** Are you going to ask the boss for more time to finish your work?
    **B:** <u>No, I'm *afraid* to ask.</u> He thinks the work is already finished!
    **a.** I don't feel comfortable asking.
    **b.** I don't need to ask.

**2** *Match the word on the left to its correct definition on the right.*

_____ 1. successful
_____ 2. owner
_____ 3. move around
_____ 4. jacket
_____ 5. material
_____ 6. hole
_____ 7. experience
_____ 8. exciting
_____ 9. advice
_____ 10. afraid

**a.** a person who has something that is his or hers

**b.** helpful ideas; suggestions

**c.** fun; making you feel happy and interested

**d.** cloth; fabric to make clothing

**e.** doing very well (in a job or at school)

**f.** to change the position of something

**g.** frightened; scared

**h.** an empty space; an opening

**i.** knowledge or skill that you get from doing a job

**j.** a short coat

# 3 LISTENING ONE: K-K Gregory, Young and Creative

## A. INTRODUCING THE TOPIC

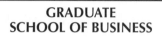

**GRADUATE
SCHOOL OF BUSINESS**

*SPECIAL LECTURE!*
"Personal Creativity in Business"
Guest speaker: K-K Gregory

9:00–11:00
Room 121
Prof. M. Ray

BUS G341
Course

**Wristies®, Inc.**

P.O. Box 577
Bedford, MA  01730-0577

*K-K Gregory*

voice     781-275-2223
fax       781-275-8120
e-mail    kk@wristies.com
web       www.wristies.com

patent pending

 *Listen to the beginning of "K-K Gregory, Young and Creative." Then circle the best answer.*

1. Who is K-K?

   **a.** a company owner
   **b.** a business student

2. Why does Professor Ray want K-K to speak to his class?

   **a.** She's a good speaker.
   **b.** The students can learn from her.

3. What will K-K talk about?

   **a.** her business
   **b.** Professor Ray's class

## B. LISTENING FOR MAIN IDEAS

🎧 *Listen to K-K Gregory. Write **T** if the sentences are true. Write **F** if the sentences are false. Correct the false information.*

_____ 1. "Wristies" cover your fingers, hands, and wrists.

_____ 2. K-K's mother helped her to make the first pair of Wristies.

_____ 3. K-K gave Wristies to her friends.

_____ 4. K-K's mother didn't have any business experience.

_____ 5. K-K and her mother were afraid to start a business.

_____ 6. K-K thinks it's good to do new things.

## C. LISTENING FOR DETAILS

🎧 *Listen again. Two answers are correct. Cross out the incorrect answer.*

1. Wristies _____.
   **a.** are made of warm material
   **b.** have a hole for the thumb
   **c.** are only for sports

2. K-K made the first pair of Wristies _____.
   **a.** because she didn't have gloves
   **b.** on a snowy day
   **c.** when she was 10

3. When K-K started the Wristies company, _____.
   **a.** she asked people for advice
   **b.** her mother had a store
   **c.** her mother helped her

4. People can buy Wristies _____.
   **a.** in department stores
   **b.** on the Internet
   **c.** at the supermarket

5. K-K thinks that having a business is _____.
   **a.** very difficult
   **b.** exciting
   **c.** creative

# D. LISTENING BETWEEN THE LINES

🎧 **1** *Listen to the excerpts from Listening One. Circle the best answers.*

### Excerpt 1

The students probably laugh because K-K _____.

    **a.** isn't telling the truth
    **b.** did something unusual
    **c.** is very funny

### Excerpt 2

K-K's mother probably helped her because she wanted K-K to _____.

    **a.** be wealthy
    **b.** stay warm
    **c.** do something exciting and creative

### Excerpt 3

The students say, "Wow!" because K-K _____.

    **a.** was on TV
    **b.** sold so many Wristies in a short time
    **c.** is exciting

**2** *Discuss these questions with the class.*

**1.** When can you wear Wristies? Think of as many activities as you can.

**2.** Did K-K's mother make a good or bad decision? Is it a good idea for children to have a business?

**3.** Do you ever buy things on TV shopping shows? On the Internet? From catalogs? Are these ways better than shopping in stores? Why or why not?

# LISTENING TWO:  A Business Class

## A. EXPANDING THE TOPIC

Professor Michael Ray,
Stanford University

🎧 **1** *Listen to Professor Ray. Circle **T** if the sentence is true. Circle **F** if the sentence is false. Professor Ray says:*

| | | |
|---|---|---|
| 1. K-K is successful because her mother helps her. | T | F |
| 2. When you're afraid, you can't be creative. | T | F |
| 3. Adults can learn from children. | T | F |
| 4. Adults are less creative than children. | T | F |
| 5. People cannot learn to be more creative. | T | F |
| 6. A meditation exercise can help students to be more creative. | T | F |

🎧 **2** *Listen again to Professor Ray and follow his directions. When you are finished, tell your story to a partner. Then discuss your stories with the class.*

## B. LINKING LISTENINGS ONE AND TWO

**1** *Read the sentences below. Who probably said each sentence? Write* **K-K Gregory, K-K's mother, Professor Ray,** *or* **student** *(in Professor Ray's class.) Discuss your answers with a partner. Are your answers the same or different?*

1. "She helped me do something exciting."          _____

2. "He's an unusual teacher."          _____

3. "It is possible to teach creativity."          _____

4. "All my friends use them in sports."          _____

5. "I believe in her. She'll be a success."          _____

6. "Adults are often afraid to make mistakes."          _____

7. "She is never afraid to do something new."          _____

**2** *Many companies want their employees to be more creative. These companies have unusual activities for employees. Here are some of the activities. Which are good ways to increase creativity? Which are not? Check (✓) the boxes.*

|  | It's a good idea. | It's *not* a good idea. | I'm not sure. |
|---|---|---|---|
| Doing exciting sports together |  |  |  |
| Studying music |  |  |  |
| Sometimes working at home |  |  |  |
| Playing games together |  |  |  |
| Learning how to do meditation |  |  |  |

*Now discuss your answers with a partner or small group.*

# 5 REVIEWING LANGUAGE

## A. EXPLORING LANGUAGE: Pronunciation of "th"

The letters *th* have two sounds:

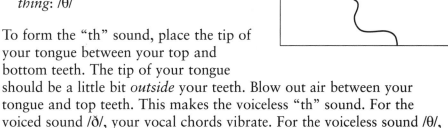

* The voiced sound in the word *this*: /ð/
* The voiceless sound in the word *thing*: /θ/

To form the "th" sound, place the tip of your tongue between your top and bottom teeth. The tip of your tongue should be a little bit *outside* your teeth. Blow out air between your tongue and top teeth. This makes the voiceless "th" sound. For the voiced sound /ð/, your vocal chords vibrate. For the voiceless sound /θ/, your vocal chords do not vibrate.

**1** *Listen to and repeat these words.*

| /ð/ | /θ/ |
|-----|-----|
| they | thanks |
| there | thought |
| that's | things |
| mother | anything |
| breathe | with |

**2** *Read these sentences and underline every word that has a "th" sound. Then read the sentences out loud to a partner. Be sure to pronounce all the "th" sounds correctly. Listen to the sentences to check your pronunciation.*

1. They're long gloves with no fingers.
2. There's a hole for the thumb.
3. Some people wear them outside; others wear them inside.
4. So then I thought, "I can sell these things!"
5. My mother didn't know anything about business.
6. You can buy them in stores and there's also a website.

**3** *Work with a partner.*

*Student A: Ask each question. Listen to your partner's answer. Is it correct? Say "That's right" or "I don't think that's right."*

*Student B: Answer each question. Use a word from the box. Does your partner agree with your answer? If your partner doesn't agree, discuss the answer.*

| anything | thinks | ~~thousand~~ |
|----------|--------|--------------|
| mother | thought | thumb |

*Read the example together for practice.*

**Example**

STUDENT A: (Question) How many Wristies did K-K sell on TV?

STUDENT B: (Answer) She sold a <u>thousand</u>!

STUDENT A: (Response) <u>That's right</u>.

1. STUDENT A: (Question) Why does K-K like business?

   STUDENT B: (Answer) She _____ it's exciting.

   STUDENT A: (Response) _____.

2. STUDENT A: (Question) Who helped K-K a lot?

   STUDENT B: (Answer) Her _____ did.

   STUDENT A: (Response) _____.

3. STUDENT A: (Question) Did K-K know a lot about business when she was 10?

   STUDENT B: (Answer) No, she didn't know _____!

   STUDENT A: (Response) _____.

4. STUDENT A: (Question) Did K-K's mother like the idea of selling Wristies?

   STUDENT B: (Answer) Yes, she _____ it was a good idea.

   STUDENT A: (Response) _____.

5. STUDENT A: (Question) Why do Wristies have a little hole?

   STUDENT B: (Answer) That's for the _____.

   STUDENT A: (Response) _____.

## B. WORKING WITH WORDS

**1** Work in pairs. Read the story below and fill in the blanks with the words from the list. Then take turns reading the story out loud.

| | | | |
|---|---|---|---|
| advice | creative | experience | successful |
| afraid | exciting | owner | |

### Trent Eisenberg, "Computer Doctor"

When Trent Eisenberg was 10 years old, he knew everything about computers. Whenever his friends or relatives had problems with their computers, they came to Trent for _____. When other people said, "It's impossible to fix this computer," Trent was never _____ to try to fix it. He usually found a new and very _____ way to fix the computer.

Trent loved to fix computers. So, when he was 14, he started his own company. Trent is the _____ of the F1 Computer Company. From the beginning, his business was very _____. He made more than $50,000 a year when he was still in high school! "Sometimes people come to me with difficult computer problems," says Trent. "When I can find the problem and fix it, they are so happy. And for me, that's very _____. I feel great!" Trent is a young man with a lot of business _____.

**2** *Work in a small group. Ask and answer these questions. Use the underlined words.*

1. Did you ever have a computer problem? Who gave you <u>advice</u>? Was it good <u>advice</u>? Why or why not?

2. What is something new that you want to do (for example, "learn a new sport," "travel to a new place")? Is it <u>exciting</u>? How do you feel? Are you <u>afraid</u>?

3. Do you know a <u>successful</u> business <u>owner</u>? What kind of business does this person own?

# SKILLS FOR EXPRESSION

## A. GRAMMAR: *There is/There are, There was/There were*

**1** *Read the conversation. Follow the instructions.*

PROFESSOR RAY:  Are there any more questions?

STUDENT:  Yes. Were there any problems in the beginning?

K-K:  Yeah, there were problems! For example, business was very slow at first because there weren't any other people in my company. There was only one person—me! Now there are three employees

1. Find and underline <u>there are, there was, there were</u> and <u>there weren't</u>.

2. Which ones talk about the present? Which ones talk about the past?

3. Find and underline <u>Are there</u> and <u>Were there</u>.

4. What word comes after <u>Are there</u> and <u>Were there</u>? Write it below.

_____

**FOCUS ON GRAMMAR**

See *there is* and *there are* in *Focus on Grammar,* Introductory.

## There is/There are, There was/There were

| | |
|---|---|
| **1.** Use *there is* or *there are* to describe something in the present. | |
| *There is* + singular count noun | **There is** one **owner**. |
| *There is* + non-count noun | **There is** a lot of **snow** on the street. |
| *There are* + plural count noun | **There are** three **employees**. |
| Use the contraction *There's* in speech or informal writing. | |
| **2.** Use *there was* or *there were* to describe something in the past. | |
| *There was* + singular count noun | **There was** one owner. |
| *There was* + non-count noun | **There was** a lot of snow. |
| *There were* + plural count noun | **There were** some problems yesterday. |
| **3.** To form a negative statement, add the contraction *n't*. | There are**n't** many employees.  There were**n't** many employees. |
| **4.** For questions, put *is/are* or *was/were* before *there*. | **Was there** a problem yesterday? |
| In *yes/no* questions, use *any* with plural nouns and non-count nouns. | **Were there any** problems?  **Was there any** snow? |

**2** *Read the interview with Andy Stefanovich, co-founder of Play. Fill in the blanks using* there + *a form of the verb* be. *Use the contraction* there's *when possible.*

ANDY: Welcome to Play! Please come in.

INTERVIEWER: Wow! This office is very unusual!

ANDY: When people come to our office for the first time, they're usually

surprised.

INTERVIEWER: Is this your meeting room?

ANDY: No, _____ any meeting rooms at Play. This is a
1. (not)

"playroom."

INTERVIEWER:  A playroom?

ANDY:  Sure. We learn to be creative from children. And children play! So this

playroom is where we create new ideas. _____ a meeting
                                              2.

in this "playroom" one hour ago. Let's look around.

INTERVIEWER:  But . . . _____ any tables or chairs in this room!
                              3. (not)

_____ really a business meeting here? Are you sure? It
        4.

looks like children were playing here. _____ balls and
                                                5.

children's toys on the floor, and _____ papers and pictures
                                          6.

on the floor and walls!

ANDY:  Those are some creative ways to get new ideas. Boring meetings give

people boring ideas. At Play meetings, the employees play! And

_____ a table in the room because we write on paper on
        7. (not)

the walls! Look over there! _____ a list on that wall of all
                                    8.

the new ideas from the meeting. Let's see. . . . _____ 10
                                                          9.

people in this room for one hour, and now _____ 50 new
                                                    10.

ideas on this list!

INTERVIEWER:  That's wonderful!

ANDY:  Yes, it is. And do you see that? _____ a special camera in
                                                11.

each playroom. The camera photographs everything that we write on

the walls.

INTERVIEWER:  This is really an unusual room!

ANDY:  Yeah. Working here is a lot of fun!


*Now read the interview out loud with a partner. Change roles and read
it again.*

## B. STYLE: Explaining How to Do Something

*Read K-K's explanation of how she made her first pair of Wristies.*

 This is how I made Wristies. First, I looked for some warm material. Then I cut it. Next, I put the material around each arm. Finally, I made a little hole for my thumb. And that's how I did it!

When we explain how to do something, or how we did something, there are usually three parts: the introduction, the steps, and the ending or summary.

**The Introduction**

You can say:

| | |
|---|---|
| *This is how I/you . . .* | **This is how I** make Wristies. |
| *This is how to . . .* | **This is how to** make Wristies. |

**The Steps**

You can say:

| | |
|---|---|
| *First/second/third, . . .* | **First,** I looked for some warm material. |
| *Then . . .* | **Then** I put it around each arm. |
| OR *Next, . . .* | OR **Next,** I put it around each arm. |
| *Finally, . . .* | **Finally,** I made a little hole for my thumb. |

**The Ending**

You can say:

| | |
|---|---|
| *And that's how I/you . . .* | **And that's how I** make Wristies. |
| *And that's how to . . .* | **And that's how to** make Wristies. |

**1** *K-K is telling how she started her business. Work with a partner. Add correct phrases from the box on page 87. Then take turns reading the story out loud.*

_____ I became a business owner. _____,
　　　　　1.　　　　　　　　　　　　　　　　　　　　2.

I made a lot of Wristies, and I gave them to all my friends as gifts.

Everybody really loved them. _____, I thought about
　　　　　　　　　　　　　　　　3.

selling them. _____, I talked to my mother about my idea.
　　　　　　　　4.

She thought it was great, so we talked to a lot of people and asked them

for business advice. _____, a few months later, I started
　　　　　　　　　　　　5.

my own company, "Wristies." _____ I became a 10-year-
　　　　　　　　　　　　　　　　6.

old business owner.

**2** *Work with a partner.*

> Student A: *Explain how to do something or how you did something. Use one of the ideas below or your own idea. Use phrases from the box on page 87.*

How to make a sandwich

How to buy a computer

How to prepare for a trip to another country

> Student B: *Listen to Student A and take notes. Make a list of the steps you hear. Then read the steps to Student A. Student A will tell you if you are correct. Then change roles.*

**Example**

**Student A**

OK, I'm going to explain how to make a peanut butter and jelly sandwich. First, take two pieces of bread. Then spread peanut butter on one piece of bread. Next, spread jelly on the peanut butter. Finally, put the other piece of bread on top of the jelly. That's how I do it.

**Student B**

1. Take two pieces of bread.
2. Spread peanut butter on one piece.
3. Spread jelly on the peanut butter.
4. Put the other piece of bread on top.

## ON YOUR OWN

### A. SPEAKING TOPICS: Creative Connections

**1** *Work in a small group. Look at the objects in the box. How can you connect them? Think of things you could make or sell.*

**Example**

STUDENT A:  I think of ties or shirts with little raindrops on them.

STUDENT B:  I think of ties or other clothes that you can wear in the rain.

**Listening Task**

*Listen to your classmates' ideas. Which idea is the best? Why?*

**2** *Listen to the music. As you listen, write the thoughts that come to your mind, or draw a picture of what you imagine. Then share your ideas with a partner. Were your ideas similar or different?*

*Discuss your ideas with the class.*

## B. FIELDWORK

**1** *Find out about a young business owner or entrepreneur (18 years old or younger). Look in the library, in business magazines, or on the Internet. Try the websites* www.wired.com *and* www.fastcompany.com. *Or tell about a young business owner that you know. Use the questions below for help.*

What is the person's name?

What is the name of this person's business?

What kind of business is it?

How old was this person when he or she started the business?

Did anyone help him or her?

Did this person have a creative idea?

Is this person successful?

Does this person have any advice for other young people?

*Give a report to the class.*

**Listening Task**

*Listen to your classmates. Ask questions. Which young business owner had the best idea?*

**2** *Watch the movie* Big, *starring Tom Hanks. In this film, 13-year-old Josh wants to be big, like an adult. His wish comes true. His body grows big, but his mind stays young. He gets a job in a toy company. Discuss the film and its connection with this unit, "Thinking Young: Creativity in Business." Begin your discussion with these questions.*

**1.** Why does the toy company owner like Josh's ideas?

**2.** Why is Josh so creative?

**3.** Why does Susan like Josh?

## FROM SADNESS TO STRENGTH

# 1 APPROACHING THE TOPIC

## A. PREDICTING

Look at the picture of Eleanor Roosevelt with children. Discuss these questions with the class.

1. Who was Eleanor Roosevelt?
2. When did she live?
3. Read the title of the unit. What does it mean?

## B. SHARING INFORMATION

**1** *Work in a small group. Look at this group of important women. Match each woman to the information about her on page 93. Write the letters on the lines.*

_____ 1. Margaret Thatcher

_____ 2. Golda Meir

_____ 3. Indira Gandhi

_____ 4. Hillary Clinton

_____ **5.** Eva (Evita) Perón     _____ **6.** Mother Teresa

**a.** She was the prime minister of India from 1966 to 1977 and 1980 to 1984. She was the first woman prime minister in the world.

**b.** She was Argentina's popular first lady from 1946 to 1952. She worked to help poor people, women, and working-class people.

**c.** She was the prime minister of England from 1979 to 1990. She was a powerful leader.

**d.** She was the prime minister of Israel from 1969 to 1974. She was a strong leader.

**e.** She was a Catholic missionary.[1] She helped sick and poor people all over the world. She won the Nobel Peace Prize in 1979.

**f.** She was the first lady of the United States from 1993 to 2001. She became a U.S. senator in 2001.

**2** *Discuss these questions with the class.*

**1.** Which women are still alive?

**2.** Were the husbands or the fathers of any of these women important men?

**3.** What other information do you know about these women?

---

[1] *missionary:* someone who goes to a foreign country to teach people about the Christian religion

# PREPARING TO LISTEN

## A. BACKGROUND

*Read the paragraphs about Eleanor Roosevelt's early life.*

Eleanor was born in 1884. She was a shy and serious child. She wasn't very pretty. Eleanor's family was rich and powerful. But Eleanor's childhood was very unhappy.

When Eleanor was 8 years old, her mother got sick and died. Her father died when she was 10. Eleanor was lonely and sad.

When Eleanor was 15, she went to school in England. There, she met Marie Souvestre, her greatest teacher. This was the happiest time in Eleanor's life. Marie Souvestre taught Eleanor how to be strong and happy. Souvestre's important lessons helped Eleanor many times in her life.

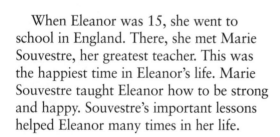

In 1902 Eleanor returned to the United States. She married Franklin Delano Roosevelt in 1905. Franklin Delano Roosevelt became president of the United States in 1933, and Eleanor became a very important woman.

*Choose the best answer to complete each sentence.*

1. As a child, Eleanor was _____.

   **a.** pretty and playful
   **b.** rich and unhappy

2. When Eleanor was a child, _____.

   **a.** both of her parents died
   **b.** her life was happy

3. Marie Souvestre helped Eleanor to become a _____.

   **a.** better student
   **b.** happier person

4. Eleanor became an important woman _____.

   **a.** when she married Franklin Delano Roosevelt
   **b.** when her husband became president of the United States

## B. VOCABULARY FOR COMPREHENSION

*Work with a partner. Read the information about Eleanor Roosevelt and Marie Souvestre. Write the correct words to complete the sentences.*

1. Marie Souvestre had her own school in England. It was called

   Allenswood. She wasn't married, and she didn't have children. In the

   early 1900s, she was not _____ woman.
   a traditional/an unusual

2. Marie Souvestre prepared her students for life. She taught them to

   think for themselves and to work hard. She wanted all women to be

   _____.
   popular/independent

**3.** Marie Souvestre's students studied world history and government.

She wanted her students to understand _____.
politics/languages

**4.** The students also studied public speaking. In class, they often had to

make short _____ about their ideas.
decisions/speeches

**5.** Marie Souvestre taught her students to explain their opinions clearly

and strongly. She said that women need to _____
speak out/be silent

in public about their ideas.

**6.** Marie Souvestre was a strong, intelligent woman and a great teacher.

All her students _____ her.
respected/helped

**7.** Eleanor had many friends at Allenswood. All the students loved her.

She was the most _____ student in the school.
beautiful/popular

**8.** After Eleanor left Allenswood, she married Franklin Delano

Roosevelt. In 1933, he became the president of the United States and

Eleanor became the _____.
first lady/vice president

**9.** Eleanor always remembered Marie Souvestre's lessons. She continued

doing _____ work all her life.
house/political

# 3 LISTENING ONE: A Very Unusual Woman, Part 1

## A. PREDICTING THE TOPIC

🎧 *Henry Samuels, the host of the radio program* Booktalk, *is interviewing Professor Jane Barlow. Professor Barlow wrote a book about Eleanor Roosevelt. Listen to the beginning of the interview. What do you think they will talk about? Circle your ideas in the list below.*

Henry Samuels and Jane Barlow will probably talk about Eleanor Roosevelt's:

1. clothes
2. work
3. friends
4. children
5. political ideas
6. travel
7. feelings
8. speeches
9. parents

## B. LISTENING FOR MAIN IDEAS

🎧 ❶ *Listen to the interview. Write* **T** *if the sentence is true. Write* **F** *if the sentence is false.*

_____ 1. In the early 1900s, many women worked in politics.

_____ 2. Eleanor didn't like political work.

_____ 3. She was a traditional first lady.

_____ 4. She made speeches about her political ideas.

_____ 5. She wanted to help many people.

_____ 6. Everybody thought Eleanor was a great woman.

❷ *Now go back to Section 3A above. Which ideas did Henry Samuels and Jane Barlow talk about?*

## C. LISTENING FOR DETAILS

🎧 *Before you listen to the interview again, circle the answer that you think is correct. Then after you listen, write the letter of the correct answer on the line.*

1. When FDR[1] was governor of New York, he couldn't _____.

    **a.** talk          **b.** walk

2. Eleanor helped her husband by traveling and making political _____.

    **a.** speeches          **b.** decisions

3. FDR became president in _____.

    **a.** 1923          **b.** 1933

4. Eleanor was very interested in helping women, children, and _____.

    **a.** poor people          **b.** men

5. She explained her political ideas on the radio and _____.

    **a.** on TV          **b.** in the newspaper

6. Some people didn't like her because she was so _____.

    **a.** popular          **b.** independent

7. When people said bad things about Eleanor, she _____.

    **a.** didn't care          **b.** got angry

## D. LISTENING BETWEEN THE LINES

🎧 **1** *Listen to the excerpts from Listening One. Circle the best title for each.*

**Excerpt 1**

   **a.** "The Beginning of Eleanor Roosevelt's Political Life"

   **b.** "The Beginning of FDR's Illness"

---

[1] "FDR" = Franklin Delano Roosevelt.

**Excerpt 2**

  **a.** "Eleanor Roosevelt's Jobs"

  **b.** "Eleanor Roosevelt's Political Opinions"

**Excerpt 3**

  **a.** "Eleanor Roosevelt: A Strong Woman"

  **b.** "Eleanor Roosevelt: A Popular Woman"

**2** *Discuss these questions with a small group.*

**1.** Why did Eleanor like making speeches?

**2.** Why did Eleanor work so hard?

**3.** Eleanor Roosevelt said that women in politics need to be very strong. Why did she say that? Do you agree with her?

# 4 | LISTENING TWO: | A Very Unusual Woman, Part 2

## A. EXPANDING THE TOPIC

 **1** *Listen to part 2 of the interview about Eleanor Roosevelt. Circle **T** if the sentence is true. Circle **F** if the sentence is false.*

**1.** Jane Barlow's book has new ideas about Eleanor Roosevelt's personal life.     T    F

**2.** Eleanor was unhappy all her life.     T    F

**3.** She was angry at FDR for a few years.     T    F

**4.** To Eleanor, marriage was the only important thing.     T    F

**5.** Marie Souvestre's lessons helped Eleanor to have an independent life.     T    F

**6.** Eleanor's life was happy only because she had important work.     T    F

**2** *Discuss these questions with the class.*

1. Why do you think Eleanor and FDR didn't get divorced?

2. Can a person in an unhappy marriage have a happy life?

## B. LINKING LISTENINGS ONE AND TWO

**1** *Work with a partner. Eleanor learned some important lessons in her life. Did she learn them* before *or* after *she became first lady? Check (✓) the correct column. Then discuss your answers with the class.*

|  | Before | After |
|---|:---:|:---:|
| 1. It's important to speak out about your ideas. | ❏ | ❏ |
| 2. When people say bad things about you, you can laugh. | ❏ | ❏ |
| 3. Women can work in politics. | ❏ | ❏ |
| 4. It's not necessary to have a happy marriage to have a happy life. | ❏ | ❏ |
| 5. A wonderful life includes good friends and important work. | ❏ | ❏ |

**2** *Discuss these questions with the class.*

1. Which experiences helped Eleanor to become a strong person?

2. Jane Barlow thinks that many male writers didn't understand Eleanor Roosevelt. Does Barlow understand Eleanor's life better because she is a woman writer?

# 5 REVIEWING LANGUAGE

## A. EXPLORING LANGUAGE: Pronunciation of -ed Endings

The past tense ending *-ed* has three different pronunciations.

**Rules**

1. If the last sound in the base verb is /d/ or /t/, *-ed* is pronounced as a separate syllable: /ɪd/.

   /ɪd/
   Eleanor want**ed** to do important things.

2. If the last sound in the base verb is /f/, /k/, /p/, /s/, /ʃ/, or /tʃ/, *-ed* is pronounced /t/.

   /t/
   Eleanor work**ed** in politics.

3. The final *-ed* is pronounced /d/ after base verbs ending in all other consonants.

   /d/
   She travel**ed** around New York.

4. If the last sound in the base verb is a vowel, *-ed* is pronounced /d/.

   /d/
   And she enjoy**ed** herself.

🎧 ① *Listen to the words. Circle the correct -ed ending.*

| | | |
|---|---|---|
| **1.** /t/   /d/   /ɪd/ | **4.** /t/   /d/   /ɪd/ | **7.** /t/   /d/   /ɪd/ |
| **2.** /t/   /d/   /ɪd/ | **5.** /t/   /d/   /ɪd/ | **8.** /t/   /d/   /ɪd/ |
| **3.** /t/   /d/   /ɪd/ | **6.** /t/   /d/   /ɪd/ | **9.** /t/   /d/   /ɪd/ |

② *Read the sentences. Look at the underlined verbs. Is -ed pronounced /t/, /d/, or /ɪd/? Write your answers above the verbs.*

/t/                    /d/
1. As time <u>passed</u>, Eleanor <u>realized</u> that she didn't want to be sad forever.

2. She <u>decided</u> that she could have a happy, independent life.

3. She <u>wanted</u> to do important work.

4. Eleanor knew that people <u>listened</u> to her when she <u>talked</u>.

5. Eleanor knew that many people in the world <u>needed</u> help.

6. So she <u>traveled</u> around the world and <u>tried</u> to help people.

7. She <u>visited</u> so many countries that people <u>called</u> her "The First Lady of the World."

8. People around the world <u>loved</u> and <u>respected</u> Eleanor Roosevelt.

**3** *Work with a partner. Compare your answers to Exercise 2. Then listen to the sentences to check your answers. Take turns reading the sentences out loud.*

## B. WORKING WITH WORDS

Martin Luther King, Jr.[1]

**1** *Read part of the* Booktalk *interview out loud with a partner. Fill in each blank with the best word from the list below.*

| | | |
|---|---|---|
| poor | respected | speech |
| political | speak out | strong |

HENRY SAMUELS:  Eleanor Roosevelt was an important American. Who was another

important American?

JANE BARLOW:  I think Martin Luther King, Jr. was also a great _____

1.

leader in the United States.

---

[1] "Jr." = Junior.

HENRY: Yes. In many ways, he was like Eleanor Roosevelt.

JANE: That's true. He always tried to help _____ people and
2.
other people who needed help. He was a great leader for African

Americans.

HENRY: And like Eleanor Roosevelt, Dr. King was a very _____
3.
person. He was never afraid to _____ about the political
4.
problems in the United States. He talked about freedom and equality all

over the country.

JANE: Yes. Today, many young Americans study his most famous

_____, "I Have a Dream," in school. The American
5.
people _____ Martin Luther King very much. Sadly, he
6.
was killed in 1968. Now his birthday is a national holiday.

**2** *Work with a partner. Ask each other the questions. Use the
underlined vocabulary in your answers.*

1. Who <u>speaks out</u> about the problems of <u>poor</u> people where you live?

2. Do you like to listen to <u>political speeches</u>? Why or why not?

3. Who was a <u>strong</u> person in history? Do you <u>respect</u> this person?
Why or why not?

# SKILLS FOR EXPRESSION

## A. GRAMMAR: Simple Past Tense

**1** *Read the conversation on page 104. Underline all the verbs that tell
about the past. Then answer the questions that follow.*

HENRY SAMUELS:   After FDR <u>died</u>, what did Eleanor Roosevelt do?

JANE BARLOW:   In 1945, Eleanor started an important career. She became U.S. delegate to the United Nations. She worked at the UN until 1951 and again from 1960 until 1962. She didn't stop working for women, children, and poor people. She helped to write the Universal Declaration of Human Rights. In 1960, at the age of 76, she wrote a book, *You Learn by Living*. In her book, she said that she loved her life because she always tried to do new things, and she always learned from her experiences. She died in 1962. The United States lost a great American that day.

### Questions

1. Which past tense verbs are regular (end in *-ed*)?

   a. _____

   b. _____

   c. _____

   d. _____

   e. _____

   f. _____

   g. _____

2. Which past tense verbs are irregular (do not end in *-ed*)?

   a. _____

   b. _____

   c. _____

   d. _____

   e. _____

   f. _____

3. Find a sentence in the negative form.

4. Find a question in the past tense.

**FOCUS ON GRAMMAR**

See the simple past of regular and irregular verbs in *Focus on Grammar,* Introductory.

## The Simple Past

**1.** Use the simple past tense to talk about actions completed in the past.

♦ To form the past tense of regular verbs, add *-ed* to the base form of the verb.

Eleanor Roosevelt travel**ed** around the world.

♦ If the base form ends in *e,* add only *-d.*

love      love*d*

The people love**d** her.

♦ If the base form ends in a consonant followed by the letter *y,* change *y* to *i* and add *-ed.*

marr*y*     marr*ied*

Eleanor marr**ied** Franklin in 1905.

---

**2.** Many verbs have irregular past tense forms.

*Note:* The simple past tense of *be* is *was* or *were,* and of *have* is *had.*

| Base Form | Simple Past |
|---|---|
| become | **became** |
| do | **did** |
| feel | **felt** |
| go | **went** |
| hear | **heard** |
| know | **knew** |
| make | **made** |
| say | **said** |
| see | **saw** |
| speak | **spoke** |
| tell | **told** |
| understand | **understood** |
| write | **wrote** |

---

**3.** To form a negative statement, use:

*didn't* + base form

Eleanor **didn't want** to be a traditional first lady.

---

**4.** To ask *yes/no* questions, use:

*Did* + subject + base form

**Did** Eleanor Roosevelt **write** a book?

---

**5.** To ask *wh-* questions, use:

*Wh-* word + *did* + subject + base form

**When did** Eleanor **become** U.S. delegate to the UN?

*Note:* If you do not know the subject of the question, do not use *did.*

**Who was** the first woman to be elected prime minister?

**2** *Read the conversation and fill in the verbs. Use the simple past tense. Then practice the conversation with a partner.*

STUDENT A: Like Eleanor Roosevelt, Hillary Clinton _____ a

                                        1. be, not

         traditional first lady. She _____ Eleanor's life and

                                           2. study

         _____ her in some ways.

             3. copy

STUDENT B: Yes, I think Hillary _____ to be like Eleanor.

                                     4. want

STUDENT A: That's true. And as first ladies, they _____ similar. Both of

                                         5. be

         them _____ families, and both of them

                    6. have

         _____ in politics.

             7. work

STUDENT B: That's right. Hillary _____ into an office in the White

                                   8. move

         House and _____ for the president.

                       9. work

STUDENT A: Also, some people _____ Hillary. And they

                            10. like, not

         _____ with her political ideas. They _____

           11. agree, not                                    12. say

         that she _____ out too much.

                13. speak

STUDENT B: Yeah. Like Eleanor, she _____ many problems in her life,

                                   14. have

         but she _____ her sadness into strength. She

                      15. turn

         _____ to have an independent life, and she

             16. decide

         _____ working in politics.

             17. stop, not

STUDENT A: You're right. In 2000, she _____ a U.S. Senator from the

                                   18. become

         state of New York.

STUDENT B:    That's another similarity. Eleanor _____ in New York, too.
                                                    **19.** live

STUDENT A:    Where in New York _____ Eleanor _____?
                                                               **20.** live

STUDENT B:    In Hyde Park, New York. _____ Hillary

_____ a book, like Eleanor did?
       **21.** write

STUDENT A:    Yes, I think she did.


## B. STYLE: Asking for Examples

When someone makes a general statement, we sometimes want more information. It's helpful to ask for an example.

JANE BARLOW:    Eleanor Roosevelt was a very unusual woman. In her time, she did things that most women didn't do.

HENRY SAMUELS:    *Like what, for example?*


JANE:    She started to speak out about her ideas.

HENRY:    *Could you give me an example?*


| |
|---|
| Could you give me an example? |
| Can you give me an example? |
| Like what, for example? |
| Like what? |

*Work with a partner.*

> *Student A: Look at this page.*
> *Student B: Look at Student Activities page 161.*
> *Student A: Read each general statement about Eleanor Roosevelt out loud. Student B will ask for an example. Choose the correct example from the list below. Read it to Student B.*

## General Statements

1. Eleanor Roosevelt did a lot of exciting things with famous friends.

2. Eleanor wrote things in the newspaper that sometimes made FDR really angry.

3. Eleanor Roosevelt made political speeches in some unusual places.

## Examples

a. She wrote a famous essay in 1938. In the essay, she disagreed with all of FDR's important international decisions.

b. Well, she took flying lessons, and once she flew a plane at night with Amelia Earhart.

c. Once she stood up during intermission at the New York Metropolitan Opera. She told the audience that they should help all the poor people in New York.

*Change roles. Listen to Student B's statements. Ask for an example. Use the questions below.*

Could you give me an example?

Can you give me an example?

Like what, for example?

Like what?

# ON YOUR OWN

## A. SPEAKING TOPICS: Talking about an Important Person

*Work with a partner. Choose topic A or B. Tell your partner about this person. Use past and present tenses. Use the questions shown below each topic to help you.*

### Topic A.  A Strong Person

Eleanor Roosevelt had a very unhappy childhood. Later she had an unhappy marriage. But she became a very successful and happy person. She turned her sadness into strength. Think of other famous people and people you know. Who is another person who turned sadness into strength?

- ◆ What is the person's name?
- ◆ Is he or she a famous person or someone you know?
- ◆ What kind of sadness did this person have?
- ◆ How did this person change his or her life? (How did the person change sadness into strength?)
- ◆ Other information?

### Topic B.  An Important Teacher

Marie Souvestre was Eleanor Roosevelt's most important teacher. When Eleanor met her, her life changed. Did you ever have a special teacher? Did a teacher ever change your life in any way?

- ◆ What was your teacher's name?
- ◆ When did you meet this teacher (in elementary school, junior high school, high school, college or university)?
- ◆ What subject did this teacher teach?
- ◆ Why was this teacher so important to you? How did this teacher change your life?
- ◆ Do you still talk or write to this teacher?
- ◆ Other information?

**Listening Task**

*Listen to your partner describe the person he or she chose. Ask your partner questions. Ask for examples.*

## B. FIELDWORK

*Choose a famous woman. Find out about her. Get information from the library or the Internet, or from people you know. Use the questions below to help. Take notes.*

When was she born?

What is/was her job?

What do you know about her work?

What do you know about her personal life?

In your opinion, why is she important?

Your questions:

_____

_____

*Give a short report to the class.*

**Listening Task**

*Listen to your classmates' reports. Ask questions. Think about the women your classmates talked about. Which woman was the most important? Why?*

## DRIVING YOU CRAZY

Picture 1                    Picture 2

# 1 APPROACHING THE TOPIC

## A. PREDICTING

Look at the pictures. Discuss these questions with the class.

1. What is happening in Picture 1? What is happening in Picture 2?
2. How do the people in each picture feel?
3. Read the title of this unit. What will the unit be about?

## B. SHARING INFORMATION

**1** *Work with a partner. Look at the pictures of driving problems. Read the sentences. Write the letter of the correct picture next to each sentence.*

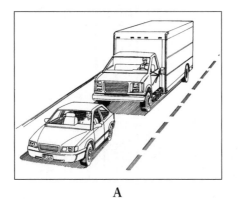

A

B

C

_____ **1.** The car is passing in the wrong lane.

_____ **2.** The truck is tailgating the car.

_____ **3.** The driver is talking on a phone and not watching the road.

*Think of other driving problems. Make a list with the class.*

**2** *Work in a small group. Discuss these questions. Then share your answers with the class.*

**1.** Do you like to drive? Why or why not?

**2.** Are some people afraid of driving? What are they afraid of?

**3.** Does driving sometimes make people angry? Why?

# PREPARING TO LISTEN

## A. BACKGROUND

**1** *Look at the report about car accidents in Millburn. Then discuss the questions.*

| CAR ACCIDENTS IN MILLBURN, JANUARY–AUGUST | |
|---|---|
| Total number of car accidents | 639 |
| Number of people hurt | 335 |
| Number of damaged[1] cars | 304 |
| Number of drunk drivers in accidents | 50 |
| Number of bicycles in accidents with cars | 47 |
| Number of pedestrians[2] in accidents with cars | 26 |
| Number of deaths | 4 |

[1]*damaged*: broken
[2]*pedestrians*: people who are walking

**1.** How many people died in car accidents?

**2.** How many people got hurt?

**3.** Which was more dangerous—walking or riding a bicycle?

**4.** How many accidents happened because of alcohol?

**2** *Read the paragraph and discuss the questions below with the class.*

People sometimes have car accidents because they do not follow traffic laws. When people break traffic laws, they sometimes have to go to traffic school. At traffic school they learn more about safe driving. They learn to be better drivers.

**1.** Do you think traffic school is a good idea? Why or why not?

**2.** When people break traffic laws, the government can also:

- Fine them (make them pay money)
- Take away their drivers' licenses
- Send them to jail

Do these things help? Why or why not?

## B. VOCABULARY FOR COMPREHENSION

*Read the conversations below. Then choose the best definition of the underlined words.*

1. **A:** I saw a bad traffic accident yesterday.
   **B:** Was anyone <u>injured</u>?
   **A:** I don't think so. I saw four people, and they all looked OK.

   <u>Injured</u> means _____.

   **a.** hurt
   **b.** angry

2. **A:** There was an accident on my street yesterday, and I called the police.
   **B:** Did the police ask for your name?
   **A:** No. You can be <u>anonymous</u> when you report an accident.

   <u>Anonymous</u> means _____.

   **a.** that other people know you
   **b.** that other people don't know you

3. **A:** Did you see that car? It almost hit us! What was that driver doing?
   **B:** I don't know. Don't worry about it. You can't <u>control</u> other drivers. You can't change their bad driving.

   To <u>control</u> other drivers means to _____.

   **a.** make them drive differently
   **b.** understand their thinking

4. **A:** I live at the corner of First Street and Broadway. It's a very dangerous <u>intersection</u>.
   **B:** Is there a street light there?
   **A:** No, but that's a good idea.

   <u>Intersection</u> means _____.

   **a.** a place where two roads cross each other
   **b.** a place where a road ends

5. **A:** Look at that driver in the car behind us. She's honking at us. Why is she so angry?
   **B:** I don't know. Why don't you go a little faster?
   **A:** I tried that, but it didn't work. How <u>rude</u>! I hate it when people honk at me.

   To be <u>rude</u> means to _____.

   **a.** act or speak in a way that is nice
   **b.** act or speak in a way that is not nice

6. **A:** I want to move to a house near my job. I don't want to drive so much.

   **B:** That's a good idea. Driving really makes you nervous. And you are already <u>stressed out</u> by your job.

   <u>Stressed out</u> means _____.

   **a.** nervous
   **b.** excited

7. **A:** I don't like to drive home after work. The roads are so <u>crowded</u>.
   **B:** I know. Everyone is going home at the same time.

   <u>Crowded</u> roads have _____.

   **a.** many cars
   **b.** noisy cars

8. **A:** I think you're a very <u>polite</u> driver. You always let the other drivers go ahead of you.
   **B:** Thanks. I try to be <u>polite</u>. I don't want to make other people angry.

   To be <u>polite</u> means to _____.

   **a.** act or speak in a way that is nice
   **b.** act or speak in a way that is not nice

# 3 LISTENING ONE:  Road Rage

## A. INTRODUCING THE TOPIC

*You will hear a teacher speaking at traffic school. He is speaking about road rage, a serious driving problem. Listen to the beginning of Road Rage. Read the questions, and discuss the answers with the class.*

1. What is road rage?

2. Why is road rage dangerous?

3. How will the true stories about road rage make the students at the traffic school feel? Check (✓) your ideas.

   _____ tired          _____ stressed out          _____ nervous

   _____ scared          _____ angry          _____ happy

## B. LISTENING FOR MAIN IDEAS

🎧 *Listen to true stories of road rage. The two speakers are John and Marie. What did each person do? Check (✓) the correct answers.*

|  | John | Marie |
|---|---|---|
| 1. Got angry | ❑ | ❑ |
| 2. Got scared | ❑ | ❑ |
| 3. Changed lanes | ❑ | ❑ |
| 4. Tailgated another car | ❑ | ❑ |
| 5. Drove into a parking lot | ❑ | ❑ |
| 6. Honked at another driver | ❑ | ❑ |

## C. LISTENING FOR DETAILS

🎧 *Listen again. Write **T** for the sentences that are true and **F** for the sentences that are false.*

_____ 1. Twelve hundred (1,200) people are injured every year because of road rage.

_____ 2. John forgot to signal when he changed lanes.

_____ 3. A driver followed John.

_____ 4. The driver hit John's car with his truck.

_____ 5. Marie was driving a red sports car.

_____ 6. Marie passed another driver.

_____ 7. Road rage happens because drivers feel stressed.

_____ 8. Fifty percent (50%) of American highways are very crowded.

_____ 9. You can learn to control other drivers.

_____ 10. Listening to the radio can make you angry.

## D. LISTENING BETWEEN THE LINES

 *Listen to the excerpts from Listening One. Then discuss these questions with the class. Explain your answers.*

**Excerpt 1**

1. How did John feel when the truck followed him?

2. How does John feel now?

3. Is John a good driver?

4. How did the truck driver feel?

**Excerpt 2**

1. How did Marie feel while she was driving?

2. How does Marie feel now?

3. Is Marie usually a polite driver?

**Excerpt 3**

1. What causes road rage?

2. How does the teacher want his students to feel?

3. Is he a good teacher? Why or why not?

# LISTENING TWO: Driving Phobia

## A. EXPANDING THE TOPIC

 *Read the paragraph.*

Road rage is one driving problem. Another driving problem is fear. When people have a very strong fear, they have a *phobia*. People with a driving phobia are afraid to drive. Some people with phobias get help from psychologists. The psychologists help them to understand and control their fear.

 **2** *Allen has a driving phobia. Listen to the conversation between Allen and his psychologist. Then complete the sentences.*

1. Allen is afraid of _____.

   **a.** driving a truck
   **b.** driving across a bridge

2. Allen is afraid that _____.

   **a.** he will hit a truck
   **b.** a truck will hit him

3. The psychologist tells him to think of other things _____.

   **a.** that he is afraid of
   **b.** that he does well

4. The psychologist tells him to _____.

   **a.** look straight ahead
   **b.** look at the water

5. In the end, Allen feels _____.

   **a.** very happy that he crossed the bridge
   **b.** a little unhappy because he didn't cross the bridge alone

## B. LINKING LISTENINGS ONE AND TWO

*Anger and fear are two problems that people have while driving. Anger and fear sometimes go together in a cycle, or circle. Look at the cycle below. Then discuss the questions in a small group.*

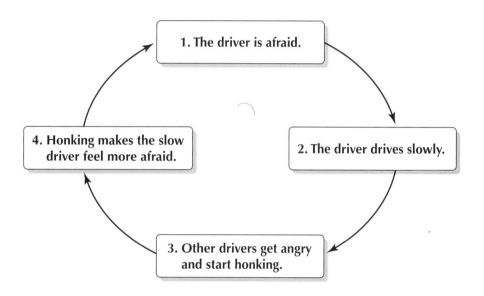

1. Think about the truck driver in John's road rage story. Imagine he is driving behind a slow driver. How does he feel? What will he do?

2. Think about Allen crossing the bridge. Imagine an angry truck driver is tailgating him. How does Allen feel? What will he do?

3. Do you sometimes change the way you drive because you are afraid? How?

# 5 REVIEWING LANGUAGE

## A. EXPLORING LANGUAGE: Syllables

Some words have only one vowel sound, or syllable. Other words have two or more syllables.

🎧 *Listen to these examples.*

honk (one syllable)

tail・gate (two syllables)

dan・ger・ous (three syllables)

In words with more than one syllable, one syllable is stressed. Stressed syllables sound longer and louder than unstressed syllables.

*Listen to the examples again. Notice the underlined syllables. These are the stressed syllables.*

🎧 **1** *Listen to the words. Write the number of syllables you hear. Then listen again and underline the stressed syllable.*

_____ **1.** rage

_____ **2.** angry

_____ **3.** story

_____ **4.** anonymous

_____ **5.** phobia

_____ **6.** intersection

**2** *Work with a partner.*

Student A: Look at this page. Say each word below.
Student B: Look at Student Activities page 162.

**1.** stress

**2.** engine

**3.** serious

**4.** traffic

**5.** dangerous

*Change roles. Listen to Student B. Write the number of syllables in each word.*

**6.** ____

**7.** ____

**8.** ____

**9.** ____

**10.** ____

## B. WORKING WITH WORDS

**1** *Work in pairs. Read the dialogue out loud.*

    *Student A: Read your sentences.*
    *Student B: Read your responses. Use the words below to*
          *complete them.*

| | | |
|---|---|---|
| anonymous | crowded | rude |
| control | get injured | stressed out |

1. **A:** Why are there so many cars today?

   **B:** It's _____ because of the holiday.

2. **A:** Are you feeling OK?

   **B:** No, I'm _____ because of the traffic.

3. **A:** Let's stop over here.

   **B:** No, there's too much traffic. It's dangerous. We could

   _____.

*Now change roles.*

4. **B:** That driver is honking her horn at you.

   **A:** I know, but I can't _____ her.

5. **B:** Are you going to yell at her?

   **A:** No, it's _____ to yell.

6. **B:** But she doesn't know you.

   **A:** You're right. I'm _____ on the road.

**2** *Discuss these questions in a small group. Use the underlined words in your answers.*

1. Why is <u>road</u> <u>rage</u> so serious?

2. Were you ever in a car accident? Were you <u>injured</u>? Who paid for a doctor?

3. What kind of driving is <u>rude</u>?

4. What kinds of things make you feel <u>stressed</u> <u>out</u>?

# SKILLS FOR EXPRESSION

## A. GRAMMAR: Comparative Adjectives

**1** *Read the sentences. Then answer the questions below.*

Marie's car is **faster than** John's car.

John is **more polite than** Marie.

1.  What is the adjective in the first sentence? What two letters does it end with?

2.  What is the adjective in the second sentence? What word comes before it?

3.  What word comes after the adjective in both sentences?

**FOCUS ON GRAMMAR**

See comparative adjectives in *Focus on Grammar,* Introductory.

### Comparative Adjectives

Use comparative adjectives + *than* to compare two people, places, or things in one sentence.

| | |
|---|---|
| 1. For adjectives with one syllable, add *-er* + *than*. | Marie's car is **faster than** John's car. |
| Add *-r* if the adjective ends in *e*. | This road is **safer than** the other road. |
| 2. For adjectives with two or more syllables, use *more* + adjective + *than*. | The roads in New York City are **more crowded than** the roads in Miami. |
| 3. For adjectives ending in *y*, change the *y* to *i* and add *-er*. | The streets in Hong Kong are **busier than** the streets in Atlanta. |
| 4. The adjectives *good* and *bad* have irregular comparative forms.<br><br>*good* → *better*<br>*bad* → *worse* | His driving is **better than** it was before.<br>Tailgating is **worse than** honking. |
| 5. You don't need *than* when the comparison is clear. | There are two roads. This road is **safer** (*safer than the other road*). |

**2** *Complete the conversations. Use the comparative form of each adjective. Then read the conversations out loud with a partner.*

1. **A:** When do you want to leave for the party?

   **B:** Let's leave early and take regular roads. The freeways are always

   _____ than the regular streets. And side streets are
   <u>crowded</u>

   usually _____.
   <u>safe</u>

2. **A:** Why is the driver behind us honking? We can't move until the

   light is green.

   **B:** I'll go out and tell him to stop.

   **A:** No, don't. That will make him _____ than he is now.
   <u>angry</u>

3. **A:** I can't believe how slow that car is going! I want to push it off

   the road!

   **B:** Hey, don't get angry. There's nothing you can do.

   **A:** I'm going to change lanes. I want to go _____.
   <u>fast</u>

4. **A:** How long does it take you to drive to work?

   **B:** About 90 minutes each way.

   **A:** Wow! I thought I had to drive a long way. But your trip is

   _____ than mine.
   <u>long</u>

5. **A:** Let's take the tunnel to go downtown.

   **B:** No, let's take the bridge. Traffic is _____ in the
   <u>bad</u>

   tunnel than on the bridge.

6. **A:** Are you happy with your new car?

   **B:** Yes, I love it. It's _____ than my old one.
   <u>comfortable</u>

**3** *Look at the information about two famous bridges. Then work in pairs. Take turns asking and answering questions. Use the adjectives below and your own ideas. Use comparatives in your questions and answers.*

new        short        old
long       colorful     tall

**Example**

STUDENT A: Which bridge is taller?

STUDENT B: The _____ is taller than the

_____.

**The Golden Gate Bridge**

**The Akashi Kaikyo Bridge**

- Goes from San Francisco to Marin County, California
- Opened in 1937
- Less than 1 mile long
- Painted red

- Height of bridge towers: 745 feet

- Goes from Honshu to Shikoku, Japan
- Opened in 1998
- More than 1 mile long
- Painted grayish white; called "Pearl Bridge"
- Height of bridge towers: 928 feet

## B. STYLE: Expressing Similar Feelings and Experiences

**1.** When we have the same feeling or experience as someone talking to us, we can use these expressions:

| | |
|---|---|
| *Me, too.* | **A:** I like driving.<br>**B: Me, too.** |
| *I do, too.* | **A:** I drive carefully.<br>**B: I do, too.** |
| *So do I.* | **A:** I listen to the radio when I drive.<br>**B: So do I.** |

**2.** If someone makes a negative statement, and we have the same feeling or experience, we can say:

| | |
|---|---|
| *I don't either.* | **A:** I don't have a car.<br>**B: I don't either** |
| *Neither do I.* | **A:** I don't like crowded roads.<br>**B: Neither do I.** |

**3.** If we have a different feeling or experience, we can say:

| | |
|---|---|
| *Oh, really? I don't.* | **A:** I like driving.<br>**B: Oh, really? I don't.** |
| *Oh, really? I do.* | **A:** I don't have a car.<br>**B: Oh, really? I do.** |

**1** *Check (✓) the sentences that are true for you. Then work with a partner.*

> *Student A: Read each statement you checked.*
> *Student B: Respond to each statement.*

**Example**
> STUDENT A:   I drive every day.
> STUDENT B:   So do I.   OR   Oh, really? I don't.

1. _____ I drive every day.

   _____ I don't drive every day.

2. _____ I often drive over the speed limit.

   _____ I don't drive over the speed limit.

3. _____ I have a driver's license.

   _____ I don't have a driver's license.

4. _____ I always use my seat belt.

   _____ I don't always use my seat belt.

*Make your own statements.*

# ON YOUR OWN

## A. SPEAKING TOPICS:
### Telling a Story

*Work in a small group. Look at the picture. Use your imaginations to answer the questions. Choose one person in your group to tell the story to the class.*

- ◆ What do you think happened?
- ◆ Why is the truck driver angry?

**Listening Task**

*Listen to all the stories. Ask one question about each story.*

## B. FIELDWORK

**1** *Observe traffic at a busy intersection. Watch the cars for 10 to 15 minutes. Count the number of dangerous drivers. Then report to the class: Where did you watch the traffic? How many dangerous drivers did you see? Why was their driving dangerous?*

**2** *Interview someone who drives. Use the questions below. Take notes. Report to the class.*

1. How do you usually drive (carefully, slowly, fast)?
2. Do you ever feel road rage?
3. Do you ever see examples of road rage?
4. Is road rage more common today than a few years ago?
5. If yes, why do you think so?
6. Are you afraid of anything when you drive?
7. (Your question)

**Listening Task**

*Listen to your classmates' reports. Is road rage a serious problem?*

# ONLY CHILD—LONELY CHILD?

Family A

Family B

## 1 APPROACHING THE TOPIC

### A. PREDICTING

Look at the pictures. Discuss these questions with the class.

1. Read the title of the unit. What does it mean? What is an *only child*?
2. How does the child in Family A feel? Why?
3. How do the children in Family B feel? Why?

## B. SHARING INFORMATION

**1** *Walk around the room. Ask your classmates the questions below. Find one student who is an only child, one who has one sibling,[1] one who has two siblings, and one who has more than two siblings. Write the information in the chart below. Then share your answers with the class.*

| Questions | Answers |
|---|---|
| Do you have any brothers or sisters? | Yes, I do./No, I don't. |
| How many brothers and sisters do you have? | I have _____ brothers and _____ sisters. |
| How old are they? | My/One brother is _____. |
| | My/One sister is _____. |

| STUDENT'S NAME | NUMBER OF SIBLINGS | AGE(S) OF SIBLINGS |
|---|---|---|
| | . . . is an only child. | |
| | . . . has one sibling. | |
| | . . . has two siblings. | |
| | . . . has more than two siblings. | |

**2** *Ask one student about his or her family. Ask these questions.*

1. Do you have any brothers or sisters?

**If the answer is *yes* . . .**

2. Are you the oldest child in your family, the youngest, or a middle child?

3. Do you get along well with your siblings or do you fight a lot?

4. (Your question)

5. (Your question)

**If the answer is *no* . . .**

2. Do you ever feel lonely? Why or why not?

3. Do you want a sibling? Why or why not?

4. (Your question)

5. (Your question)

---

[1] *sibling:* brother or sister

# PREPARING TO LISTEN

## A. BACKGROUND

*Look at the graphs. Then answer the questions below.*

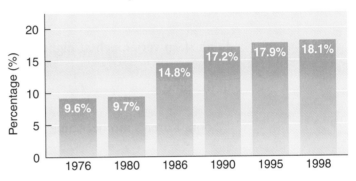

**GRAPH 1  Percentage of U.S. Women Aged 40–44 Who Have Only One Child, 1976–1998**

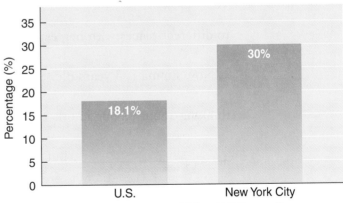

**GRAPH 2  Percentage of U.S. Families with Only One Child in the United States and in New York City, 1999**

*Source:* Data for Graphs 1 and 2 from U.S. Census Bureau.

1. Look at Graph 1. Is the number of only children in the United States going up or going down? Why is this happening? Is it happening where you live?

2. Look at Graph 2. How are families in New York City different from families in the rest of the United States? Why? Where you live, is family size different in the city and in the countryside?

## B. VOCABULARY FOR COMPREHENSION

*Read the story. Choose the best word or phrase to complete each sentence. Then take turns reading the sentences out loud with a partner.*

Karen and Ron fell in love and _____ when they
　　　　　　　　　　　　　　　　　　　　　1. got married/got lost

were both 28. When Karen was 30, she _____. Karen
　　　　　　　　　　　　　　　　　　　　　　　　2. had a child/found a child

and Ron named their daughter Emma. Emma was a happy baby, but she

didn't sleep very much at night, so Karen was _____
　　　　　　　　　　　　　　　　　　　　　　　　　　　　　3. lonely/tired

all the time.

　　Soon, Karen's mother came to live with her. She is helping Karen and

Ron to _____ their daughter. Karen and Ron both
　　　　　　4. have/raise

work, so they are very _____ during the week. But
　　　　　　　　　　　　　　5. busy/happy

on the weekends, they love to _____ Emma and go
　　　　　　　　　　　　　　　　　　6. spend time with/visit

to different places with her, especially the park and the zoo.

　　Now Emma is 3 years old. She is an only child. Karen and Ron are

thinking about having another child. They would like Emma to have a

_____. But they are worried. They want to give
　　　　7. sibling/parent

Emma a good life. But today everything is so _____!
　　　　　　　　　　　　　　　　　　　　　　　　8. wealthy/expensive

Do they have enough money for two children? They're not sure.

# 3 LISTENING ONE: Changing Families

## A. INTRODUCING THE TOPIC

The Family Network
presents

*Changing
Families*

with
Maria
Sanchez

🎧 *Listen to the beginning of* Changing Families. *Then complete the sentences below.*

**1.** You are listening to a _____.

   **a.** TV interview show

   **b.** TV drama

**2.** Maria is probably going to ask the parents, "Why did you decide to _____?"

   **a.** have only one child

   **b.** become parents

**3.** What are Maria and the parents going to talk about? Check (✓) your ideas.

| | | | |
|---|---|---|---|
| _____ **a.** siblings | _____ **f.** teachers |
| _____ **b.** culture | _____ **g.** grandparents |
| _____ **c.** decisions | _____ **h.** travel |
| _____ **d.** money | _____ **i.** friends |
| _____ **e.** age | _____ **j.** television |

## B. LISTENING FOR MAIN IDEAS

🎧 *Listen to the interview. Complete the sentences with the best words from the list. (You will not need to use all the words.)*

| | | |
|---|---|---|
| busy | a good job | more |
| difficult | a good life | old |
| easy | lonely | siblings |
| fewer | money | young |

1. Today, there are _____ only children than in the past.

2. Marion and Mark think that raising a young child is

   _____.

3. Marion and Mark think that they are too _____ to have more children.

4. Marion and Mark think that Tonia is not _____.

5. Tom and Jenna don't make a lot of _____.

6. Tom and Jenna want their son to have _____.

7. Jay is a(n) _____ kid.

## C. LISTENING FOR DETAILS

🎧 *Listen again. Write **T** for the sentences that are true and **F** for the sentences that are false.*

_____ 1. There are many only children in big cities.

_____ 2. Marion had a baby when she was 38.

_____ 3. Tonia spends time with her parents and relatives.

_____ 4. Tonia is a popular girl.

_____ 5. Maria heard that many only children are lonely.

_____ 6. Tom and Jenna love children.

_____ 7. School, music, and travel are important to Tom and Jenna.

_____ 8. Sometimes Jay has nothing to do.

# D. LISTENING BETWEEN THE LINES

**1** *Listen to the excerpts from Listening One. Choose the best answers.*

### Excerpt 1

Marion and Mark probably think that younger parents _____.

- **a.** are not so tired
- **b.** are always tired

### Excerpt 2

Mark thinks this information is _____.

- **a.** surprising
- **b.** not true

### Excerpt 3

Tom and Jenna want their son to _____.

- **a.** be the best child
- **b.** have the best life

**2** *Discuss these questions with the class.*

1. Why is it good to be an older parent? Why is it good to be a younger parent? Which is better?

2. Are only children usually more popular than children with siblings? Are they more intelligent? Explain your answers.

3. Do parents need a lot of money when they have children? Why or why not?

# 4 LISTENING TWO: How Do Only Kids Feel?

## A. EXPANDING THE TOPIC

🎧 *Listen to Tonia and Jay speaking to Maria Sanchez. Then complete the sentences.*

1. Tonia _____ being an only child.

   a. likes
   b. loves
   c. doesn't like

2. Most of Tonia's friends have _____.

   a. siblings
   b. sisters
   c. older parents

3. Tonia's parents _____ their decision to Tonia.

   a. didn't explain
   b. explained
   c. aren't going to explain

Tonia

4. How does Tonia feel about her parents' decision? She _____.

   a. understands it and agrees with it
   b. understands it but isn't happy about it
   c. doesn't understand it

5. Jay and Tonia have _____ feelings about being only children.

   a. unusual
   b. the same
   c. different

Jay

6. When Jay spends time with his parents, he feels _____.

   **a.** different
   **b.** special
   **c.** uncomfortable

7. Jay and his parents enjoy _____.

   **a.** traveling
   **b.** living in Colorado
   **c.** staying home

8. Many of Jay's friends don't have _____.

   **a.** parents
   **b.** siblings
   **c.** families

## B. LINKING LISTENINGS ONE AND TWO

**1** *Discuss these questions with the class.*

1. Do Tonia's parents understand her feelings about being an only child?

2. What can Tonia learn from Jay? What can Tonia's parents learn from Jay's parents?

**2** *Discuss this question with a small group.*

Why do some parents decide to have only one child?

*Think of reasons from Listenings One and Two. Think of your own reasons. Write the reasons below. Share your reasons with the class.*

**Reasons from Listenings One and Two**

1. The parents are too old.
2. _____
3. _____

**Other Reasons (your ideas)**

1. There are too many people in the world.
2. _____
3. _____

**3** *Discuss these questions with the class.*

1. Which reasons in Exercise 2 do you agree with? Which reasons do you disagree with? Why?

2. Do you think it's good to have only one child? Why or why not?

## REVIEWING LANGUAGE

### A. EXPLORING LANGUAGE: *Be going to*

We use *be going to* + verb to talk about the future, especially future plans:

I'*m going to take* piano lessons in October.

*Going to* can be pronounced two ways:

◆ In informal or normal speech, use the reduced form:
*gónna* /gə́nə/

◆ In very formal or careful (slow) speech, use the full form:
*going to* /gówɪŋ tə/

*Note:* We usually do not write *gonna*. *Gonna* is used in speaking.

**1** *Listen to these sentences. Is* going to *pronounced in the full form or the reduced form* (gonna)? *Circle your answer. First, listen to the examples.*

**Examples**

TONIA: But my mom said, "I am not _____ have another child."
     (a.) going to
     b. gonna

MARIA: Today, we're _____ talk about only children.
     a. going to
     (b.) gonna

**1.** MARIA: Today, we are _____ meet two families with only children.

    **a.** going to
    **b.** gonna

**2.** MARIA: First, we're _____ talk with Marion and Mark Gold.

    **a.** going to
    **b.** gonna

**3.** MARIA: OK, next, I'm _____ talk to the kids!

    **a.** going to
    **b.** gonna

**4.** MARIA: We're _____ speak to Marion and Mark's daughter, Tonia.

    **a.** going to
    **b.** gonna

**5.** JAY: Like, this year, we're _____ go skiing in Colorado.

    **a.** going to
    **b.** gonna

**2** *Match the phrases in Column A and Column B to make true sentences about you and the people in your family. With a partner, take turns saying your sentences out loud using the reduced form (gonna). Then share some of your sentences with the class.*

**Example**

STUDENT 1: "I'm not *gonna* have a big family."

STUDENT 2: "I'm *gonna* travel this year."

| A | B |
|---|---|
| **1.** I'm (not) going to | **a.** travel this year. |
| **2.** My (wife/husband) is probably (not) going to | **b.** have just one child. |
| **3.** My (mother/father) is probably (not) going to | **c.** have a big family. |
| **4.** My (brother/sister) is probably (not) going to | **d.** take a vacation this year. |
| **5.** My parents are (not) going to | **e.** have a baby soon. |
| | **f.** go skiing next winter. |
| | **g.** get married in a few years. |
| | **h.** be busy tonight. |

## B. WORKING WITH WORDS

*Work in pairs.*

> *Student A: Read the sentences out loud.*
> *Student B: Read the sentences out loud. Choose the correct*
>   *words from the list.*

busy      spent      time
raise      tired

STUDENT A:   Did your parents work when you were a child?

STUDENT B:   Yes, but my grandmother lived with us. She helped to

_____ me.
          1.

STUDENT A:   Really? That's so unusual . . .

STUDENT B:   Yeah, but it was great because my parents were always so

_____ with their jobs.
          2.

STUDENT A:   Oh . . .

STUDENT B:   They came home late, and then they were really _____.
                                                          3.

STUDENT A:   So your grandmother took care of you?

STUDENT B:   Yeah. She always had time to talk and play. We _____ a

lot of _____ together.
          4.

STUDENT A:   You were a lucky kid!

STUDENT B:   Yes, I think so.

> *Student B: Read the sentences out loud.*
> *Student A: Read the sentences out loud. Choose the correct*
>   *words from the list.*

decide         have (a child)      only children
got married    kid                 sibling

STUDENT B:   Did I tell you the news about my sister, Joan?

STUDENT A:   Is she going to _____ a baby?
                            5.

STUDENT B:   Yes, I'm so excited!

STUDENT A:   That's wonderful! But she and David just _____ six
                                                     6.

months ago.

STUDENT B:    I know.

STUDENT A:    Why did they _____ to start a family so soon?
7.

STUDENT B:    Well, Joan is 42, you know, so they didn't want to wait.

STUDENT A:    Oh, I can understand that. I guess they really want to have a

_____ .
8.

STUDENT B:    You mean *kids*. They want to have *two* children.

STUDENT A:    Yeah, a lot of parents want their child to have a _____ .
9.

STUDENT B:    Uh-huh . . . she said she doesn't want her child to feel lonely.

STUDENT A:    But you know, _____ are not always lonely!
10.

STUDENT B:    That's true.

# 6 SKILLS FOR EXPRESSION

## A. GRAMMAR : The Future with *Be going to*

**1** *Tonia is talking to Jay after the TV show. Read the dialogue. Look at the underlined verbs. Then answer the questions below.*

JAY:   I'm going to have lunch with my parents. How about you?
TONIA:   We are going to visit my grandparents.

1. How many parts does each verb have?

2. What is the first part?

3. What is the second part? Does it change?

4. What's the form of the last part?

## FOCUS ON GRAMMAR

See the future with *be going to* in *Focus on Grammar,* Introductory.

## The Future with *Be going to*

| | |
|---|---|
| **1.** Use *be* + *going to* + the base form of the verb to talk about an action in the future. | I **am going to have** lunch with my parents tomorrow.<br><br>She **is going to** visit her friends tonight. |
| *Note:* Use contractions in speaking and informal writing. | I**'m going to** have lunch.<br>They**'re going to** visit us. |
| **2.** To make a negative sentence, put *not* before *going to*. | I'm **not going to** travel.<br>He's **not going to** have a big family. |
| *Note:* You can use the negative contractions *isn't* and *aren't*. | He **isn't going to** get married soon.<br>We **aren't going to** be lonely. |
| **3.** To make *yes/no* questions, put a form of *be* before the subject. | **Are you** going to visit your grandparents soon?<br>**Is he** going to buy a car next year? |
| **4.** You can use these future time expressions with *be going to*:<br><br>tonight<br>tomorrow<br>in a week<br>in two days<br>this month<br>next year<br>soon | I'm going to get married **next year.**<br>We're going to have dinner together **tonight.** |

**2** *Tonia is talking about her plans for the future. Complete the dialogue with the correct forms of* be going to. *Then read the dialogue out loud with a partner.*

1. MARIA: I know you don't like being an only child.

   _____ you _____ have a big

   family when you grow up?

2. TONIA: Definitely! I _____ have four or five kids!

   Maybe six!

3. MARIA: Well, then your children _____

   _____ be lonely! That's for sure!

4. TONIA: Right. They _____ have a lot of brothers and

   sisters to play with.

5. MARIA: But, you know, raising so many kids is very expensive!

6. TONIA: Well, I _____ work hard and save a lot of

   money. I _____ be rich!

7. MARIA: What a plan! You're only eight years old and you already

   know that you _____ be rich! That's amazing!

**3** *Work with a partner. Use the verbs in column A and/or the time expressions in column B to ask and answer questions.*

| A | B |
|---|---|
| go shopping | this year |
| take a vacation | next week |
| move to a different city | in a month |
| move to the countryside | soon |
| see a movie | tonight |
| visit a good friend | tomorrow |
| buy a car | |
| have a big family | |

**Examples**

Are you going to move to a different city this year?
Are you going to see a movie tonight?

## B. STYLE: Explaining Reasons with *Because*

**Because**

Use *because* to give a reason. *Because* answers the question "Why?"

| | |
|---|---|
| When Tonia explains why she wants a sister, she uses *because*. | I want a sister **because** I hate being an only child. |

**1** *Match the fact in column A with the reason in column B. Write the correct letter on each line.*

**A**

_____ 1. Tonia's going to have a big family

_____ 2. Some children feel lonely

_____ 3. Jay's going to go to Colorado

**because**

**B**

a. they don't have any siblings.

b. he wants to go skiing.

c. she thinks children need siblings.

**2** *Work with a partner. Match the fact in column A with the reason in column B. Use because to connect the two parts. Take turns reading the sentences out loud.*

**A**

_____ 1. Jay is very lucky

_____ 2. Tonia feels different from her friends

_____ 3. Tonia's mother isn't going to have another child

_____ 4. Jay is never lonely

_____ 5. Tonia is unhappy

**because**

**B**

a. they all have siblings.

b. she feels too old.

c. his parents take him on a lot of vacations.

d. she wants a sister.

e. he has a lot of friends.

**3** *Work with a partner. Take turns asking and answering questions with because. See the example on page 143.*

**Example**

> **A:** Why do some only children feel lucky?
> **B:** They feel lucky because their parents spend a lot of time with them.

1. **A:** Is it good to be the oldest child in a family? Why or why not?
   **B:** It's good/it's not good . . .

2. **B:** Is it better to be the middle child or the youngest child in a family? Why?
   **A:** It's better to be . . .

3. **A:** Why do many parents worry about their only children?
   **B:** Many parents . . .

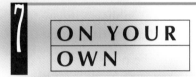

# ON YOUR OWN

## A. SPEAKING TOPIC: "An Important Decision"

*Read the situation and follow the steps below. Work with a group. Then work with a partner.*

Michael and Ellen are married. Michael is 30 years old. He works full-time. Ellen is 31 and works part-time. They have a 3-year-old son named Sam. Michael wants to have another child. Ellen isn't sure. They live in a small apartment in a big city. They pay a lot of money for rent.

**Prepare:** Group 1: You are Michael. Make a list of reasons why you may want to have another child.

Group 2: You are Ellen. Make a list of reasons why you may not want to have another child.

**Role-play:** Work with a partner from the other group. Role-play a conversation between Michael and Ellen. Use the reasons on your lists. Try to make a decision about having another child.

**Discuss:** Share your decisions with the class. How many pairs decided to have another child? How many decided not to?

**Listening Task**

*Listen to your classmates. Ask questions. Do you agree with "Michael" or "Ellen"?*

## B. FIELDWORK

**1** *Interview a friend, neighbor, or teacher. Ask the questions below. Take notes. You can begin like this:*

"May I ask you some questions about your family?"

OR

"Do you mind if I ask you some questions about your family?"

**Questions**

1. Do you have any brothers or sisters?

| **If the answer is *no* . . .** | **If the answer is *yes* . . .** |
|---|---|
| 2. Did you like being an only child when you were younger? Do you like it now? Why or why not? | 2. How many siblings do you have? What are their names? |
| 3. What's the best thing about being an only child? What's the worst thing? | 3. Are you the oldest, the youngest, or a middle child? |
| 4. Why did your parents decide to have only one child? Do you know their reason? | 4. When you were a child, did you like being the oldest? The youngest? A middle child? Why or why not? |
| 5. Did you ever feel lonely as a child? | 5. What was the best thing about being the oldest? The youngest? A middle child? What was the worst thing about it? |
| 6. Who did you play with? | 6. Did you have a good relationship with your siblings when you were children? How about now? |
| 7. (Your question) _____ | 7. (Your question) _____ |

**2** *Work in groups of three students. Give a short report about the person you interviewed.*

**Listening Task**

*Listen to your classmates' reports. Ask each student three questions about the person he or she interviewed.*

# THE QUIZ SHOW

## 1 APPROACHING THE TOPIC

### A. PREDICTING

Look at the pictures. Discuss these questions with the class.

1. What are *Wheel of Fortune* and *Jeopardy*?
2. What can people win?

## B. SHARING INFORMATION

*Work in a small group. Ask each other the following questions. Choose one student to tell your group's answers to the class.*

**1.** Do you watch TV game shows? What shows?
**2.** Do you play Scrabble or other word games? What games?
**3.** Do you enter contests? What contests?
**4.** Do you play games to win money? What games?

# PREPARING TO LISTEN

## A. BACKGROUND

*Read the information about TV quiz shows in the 1950s. Then discuss the questions that follow with the class.*

In the 1950s, television was new in the United States. Families and neighbors enjoyed watching TV together. TV game shows became popular at this time. In fact, there were 22 game shows on TV during the 1950s. One popular game show was *The $64,000 Question*. People loved to watch this show. Forty-seven million people watched it every Sunday night. *The $64,000 Question* was called a quiz show because players had to answer difficult questions to win. Other popular quiz shows in the 1950s were *Twenty-One* and *Tic Tac Dough*.

However, at the end of the 1950s, there was a quiz show scandal.[1] Some players got the answers to the questions before the show. This helped them to win. Many people were upset when they found out that some of the quiz shows were not real games. They thought that everything they saw on TV game shows was real and true.

**1.** How did people win money on *The $64,000 Question*?
**2.** Why were people unhappy with quiz shows at the end of the 1950s?
**3.** Do you know any TV game shows? How can people win money on these shows?

---

[1] *scandal:* something that people think is bad, not true, or very surprising

## B. VOCABULARY FOR COMPREHENSION

*Read the sentences. Then match the words and the definitions below.*

1. My grandmother's <u>favorite</u> game show is *The Price Is Right*. She watches it every day.

2. Yesterday, she told me that the <u>champion</u> won $20,000 and a car. The other player won $2,000.

3. There were three <u>contestants</u> on *Wheel of Fortune*—two women and one man.

4. One player was really <u>smart</u>. She knew all the answers.

5. There are so many restaurants in this city. We can eat a different type of <u>cuisine</u> every night of the week! My favorite is Chinese.

6. I love <u>spicy</u> foods, but after I eat them I usually have to drink a lot of water.

7. Sometimes questions on game shows are very <u>hard</u> and no one knows the answer.

8. One player got very easy questions. The other one got very difficult questions. That's not <u>fair</u>.

9. When you know the answer to a question, you can answer it <u>correctly</u>.

10. Some game shows are really <u>strange</u>. On one show the players have to wear really funny clothes.

| | | |
|---|---|---|
| _____ 1. favorite | **a.** intelligent; well-educated |
| _____ 2. champion | **b.** having a strong, usually hot, taste |
| _____ 3. contestant | **c.** different; unusual |
| _____ 4. smart | **d.** liked more than others |
| _____ 5. cuisine | **e.** the winner of a game |
| _____ 6. spicy | **f.** difficult |
| _____ 7. hard | **g.** done the right way with no mistakes |
| _____ 8. fair | **h.** type of cooking |
| _____ 9. correctly | **i.** player; someone who plays a game |
| _____ 10. strange | **j.** equal for everyone |

# 3 LISTENING ONE: What in the World?

## A. INTRODUCING THE TOPIC

🎧 *Listen to Christina and Emily talking about a TV show. Then read the questions. Check (✓) your answers.*

**1.** What kind of show is *What in the World?*

\_\_\_\_ a news show

\_\_\_\_ a game show

\_\_\_\_ a movie

**2.** What will you probably hear next?

\_\_\_\_ music

\_\_\_\_ different languages

\_\_\_\_ questions

\_\_\_\_ a news report

\_\_\_\_ names of winners

\_\_\_\_ a speech

\_\_\_\_ (Your idea) _____

## B. LISTENING FOR MAIN IDEAS

🎧 **1** *Read the sentences. Then listen. Circle the best answers.*

1. Christina and Emily are _____.

   **a.** friends
   **b.** sisters
   **c.** mother and daughter

2. Last week Mr. Smith _____.

   **a.** lost the game
   **b.** won the game
   **c.** won $500

3. The questions are about international _____.

   **a.** languages
   **b.** movies
   **c.** food

4. Mr. Smith _____ the answer to the first question.

   **a.** knew
   **b.** didn't know
   **c.** wasn't sure of

5. Professor Johnson _____ the answer to the second question.

   **a.** knew
   **b.** didn't know
   **c.** didn't say

6. Mr. Smith _____ the last question.

   **a.** answered
   **b.** didn't understand
   **c.** didn't answer

**2** Go back to Section 3A, item 2, on page 148. Were your ideas correct?

## C. LISTENING FOR DETAILS

🎧 *Listen again. Read the sentences and circle* TRUE *or* FALSE. *Correct the sentences that are false.*

| | | |
|---|---|---|
| 1. Both women wanted to watch the game show. | TRUE | FALSE |
| 2. The first question was about Mexican food. | TRUE | FALSE |
| 3. Contestants get $10,000 for each correct answer. | TRUE | FALSE |
| 4. The second question was about Chinese food. | TRUE | FALSE |
| 5. One sister thought that the second question was too hard. | TRUE | FALSE |
| 6. Mr. Smith will leave the show if he gives the correct answer. | TRUE | FALSE |
| 7. Mr. Smith won $6,000. | TRUE | FALSE |
| 8. The other sister thought the last question was too easy. | TRUE | FALSE |

## D. LISTENING BETWEEN THE LINES

🎧 ① *Listen to the excerpts from Listening One. Then read the questions and choose the correct answers. Discuss your answers with the class.*

**Excerpt 1**

What does Emily think about the new contestant?

    a. She thinks he's going to do well.
    b. She thinks he will not do well.

**Excerpt 2**

What does Christina think about the first question?

    a. She thinks it's a good one.
    b. She thinks it's not a good one.

**Excerpt 3**

1. How does Mr. Smith feel about the question?

    a. He thinks it's easy.
    b. He thinks it's difficult.

**2.** How does Professor Johnson feel about the question?

   **a.** He thinks it's easy.
   **b.** He thinks it's difficult.

**3.** What does Emily think about the show?

   **a.** She thinks it's fair.
   **b.** She thinks it's not fair.

**2** *Discuss these questions with the class.*

*In your opinion:*

> Was the first question easy or difficult?
>
> Was the last question easy or difficult?
>
> Do you think the game was fair?

# LISTENING TWO: "A Quiz Show Scandal"

## A. EXPANDING THE TOPIC

**1** *Listen to a news report. Look at the picture of Professor Johnson. Write short answers to the questions below. Discuss them with a partner.*

**1.** Look at the headline. What is a quiz show scandal?

**2.** What do you think Professor Johnson is going to talk about?

**3.** How do you think he feels? Why?

*Listen to the news report "A Quiz Show Scandal," and check your answers.*

**2** *Read the sentences. Check (✓) the sentences that are true.*

_____ 1. *What in the World?* was not a real game.

_____ 2. Only Professor Johnson knew the right answers before he played.

_____ 3. People wanted to see the same players win every time.

_____ 4. Professor Johnson will not keep the money he won.

_____ 5. *Truth in Television* is a new game show.

**3** *Discuss this question with the class:*

What should the game show players do with their money? Should they keep it or give it away? Why?

**4** *Think about shows you watch on television. Which shows are "real"? Which shows are not? How are they different?*

## B. LINKING LISTENINGS ONE AND TWO

*Answer the questions. More than one answer is possible. Then work in a small group and compare your answers.*

1. Do you think people wanted Professor Johnson to win?

_____ Yes _____ No _____ Maybe

Reason: _____

2. How will Christina and Emily feel when they hear Professor Johnson's announcement?

_____ Surprised _____ Not surprised _____ Angry _____ Other

Reason: _____

3. How do you think the other quiz show players feel about Professor Johnson's announcement?

_____ Surprised _____ Angry _____ Sad _____ Other

Reason: _____

# 5 REVIEWING LANGUAGE

## A. EXPLORING LANGUAGE: Intonation

When we ask *wh-* questions (*what, when, where, who, why, how*), we use falling intonation. At the end of a *wh-* question our voice falls (gets lower).

🎧 *Listen.*

What is jalapeño?

Where do people eat rice?

Who are the contestants?

Where do people use chopsticks?

🎧 **1** *Listen and repeat the questions.*

1. What is your favorite game show?
2. When is it on television?
3. Who is the host[1]?
4. How do the contestants win money?
5. Why are game shows fun to watch?
6. Where are game shows popular?

**2** *Work in pairs.*

> Student A: Ask the questions from Exercise 1.
> Student B: Answer the questions.

*Now change roles.*

---

[1] *host:* the person who talks to the contestants and asks the questions

## B. WORKING WITH WORDS

*Work with a partner. Ask each other the questions below. Use the underlined vocabulary in your answers.*

1. Which is easier for you—taking a <u>quiz</u> or writing a paper?
2. What part of English grammar is <u>hard</u> for you?
3. Who is your <u>favorite</u> actor on television?
4. Do you know a <u>strange</u> television show? What is it?
5. Imagine that a student doesn't come to class on the day of the test. The teacher gives the student the test the next day. Is this <u>fair</u>?

*Work in a small group. Ask and answer these questions. Use the underlined words in your answers.*

6. What is your <u>favorite cuisine</u>?
7. Do you like <u>spicy</u> food? Give an example.
8. Would you like to be a <u>contestant</u> on a game show? Why or why not?
9. Did your teacher ever ask you a <u>hard</u> question? What was it? Did you know the answer?

# 6 SKILLS FOR EXPRESSION

## A. GRAMMAR: *Should*

**1** *Read the sentences and answer the question.*

> You *should* watch the show. It's great.
> The contestants *should* give the money back.

When do we use *should*? (Two answers are correct.)

   **a.** To give advice
   **b.** To talk about difficult things you can or can't do
   **c.** To talk about a good thing to do

**2** *Ask a partner: What does* should *mean in the first sentence? What does it mean in the second sentence?*

## FOCUS ON GRAMMAR

See *should* in *Focus on Grammar,* Introductory.

### Should

Use *should* to give someone advice or to talk about a good thing to do.

| | |
|---|---|
| **1.** For affirmative sentences, use: *should* + the base form of the verb | She **should watch** the TV show. It's great. He **should give** the money back to them. |
| **2.** For negative sentences, use: *shouldn't* + the base form of the verb | He **shouldn't keep** the money. We **shouldn't** watch the show. |
| **3.** To ask *yes/no* questions, put *should* before the subject. | **Should we watch** TV during dinner? |
| **4.** To ask *wh-* questions, put the *wh-* word and *should* before the subject. | **What should Professor Johnson do** with the money? |

**③** *Read the conversation about the real quiz show scandal. Write* should *or* shouldn't *in the blanks.*

Charles Van Doren on the quiz show *Twenty-One*

**A:** Did you watch the news?

**B:** Um . . . no, I didn't. I was busy.

**A:** You _____ watch the news more often. It's
　　　　　　　　1.
important.

**B:** You're right. I _____ . What happened?
　　　　　　　　　　　2.

**A:** Well, do you know the quiz show *Twenty-One*? Do you

remember Charles Van Doren?

**B:** Sure. Wasn't he the champion for 14 weeks?

**A:** Yes, but on the news they said that he knew all the questions and the answers before each show. So it wasn't a real game.

**B:** That's not fair! They _____ put that kind of show
3.
on TV.

**A:** I agree with you. He won $129,000. I think he

_____ give the money back. He
4.

_____ keep it.
5.

**B:** What _____ we think when we watch *Twenty-One*
6.
now?

**A:** Well, it's not just *Twenty-One*. The news said some other quiz shows were not real games. _____ we stop
7.
watching them?

**B:** Maybe we _____ . I can't believe anything I see on
8.
TV now!

**4** *Work in pairs. Read the conversation out loud. Then change roles.*

## B. STYLE: Responding to Questions

> When you answer questions, sometimes you need time to think. When you are not sure of the answer or need more time to think, you can say:
>
> Uh, let me think . . .          Ummm . . .
>
> Um, I'm not sure . . .          Mmm, hold on . . .

*Work in pairs.*

> *Student A: Ask four questions about English. Ask about pronunciation, spelling, past tense, and meaning.*
> *Student B: Answer the questions, using expressions from the box.*

*Now change roles.*

**Example**

**A:** (Pronunciation) How do you pronounce the word S-P-I-C-Y?

**B:** Uh, let me think . . . /spaɪ siy/

**A:** (Spelling) How do you spell the word *quiz*?

**B:** Um, I'm not sure. . . . I think it's Q-U-I-Z.

**A:** (Past tense) What's the past tense of the word *run*?

**B:** Mmm, hold on . . . I think it's *ran*.

**A:** (Meaning) What does the word *champion* mean?

**B:** Ummm . . . it means "winner."

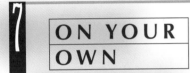

# ON YOUR OWN

## A. SPEAKING TOPICS: Categories

**①** *Play the game "Categories."*

**Step 1:** *Work in groups of four. Read the four topics or categories below. Try to think of at least two questions about each topic. You can use information you have read about in this book or use your own ideas. Write each question and answer on a small piece of paper.*

| Categories | Example Questions and Answers |
|---|---|
| Places | Where is Oxford University? (*England*) |
| Famous People | Who was Indira Gandhi? (*Prime Minister of India*) |
| English Words | How do you spell *experience*? (*e-x-p-e-r-i-e-n-c-e*) |
| Television and Movies | Who is the host of Wheel of Fortune? (*Pat Sajak*) |

**Step 2:** *Take turns asking and answering questions with another group of students. If a student answers correctly, the group gets one point. If a student answers incorrectly, the group does not get a point. The group with the most points at the end of the game wins.*

**②** *Work with a partner. Tell your partner about a game show in your country.*

**Listening Task**

*Listen to your partner describe a game show. Ask your partner questions. Would you like to watch the game show? Why or why not?*

## B. FIELDWORK

**1** *Watch a TV game show. As you watch, answer these questions. Take notes. Give a short oral report to the class or a small group.*

1. What is the name of the show?
2. Who is the host?
3. How many contestants are there?
4. What do the contestants win?
5. How exciting is the game show? (Circle one.)

    *Not exciting*      *A little exciting*      *Very exciting*

    Explain: _____

6. How surprising is the game show? (Circle one.)

    *Not surprising*      *A little surprising*      *Very surprising*

    Explain: _____

7. Are the prizes good? (Circle one.)

    *Not very good*      *OK*      *Very good*

    Explain: _____

**2** *Answer these questions with the class or in a small group.*

1. Do you think that everything is real and fair on these shows? Or do you think the players know what is going to happen before they play? Explain.
2. Would you like to play any of these game shows? Why or why not?
3. Should the prizes be different? Why or why not?

**Listening Task**

*Listen to your classmates' reports. Which show do you think is the best? Why?*

**3** *Watch the movie* Quiz Show. *It tells the story of the scandal about the quiz show* Twenty-One *and* Charles Van Doren. *Discuss the film. Then discuss the following questions with the class.*

1. How are game shows different today? How are they similar?
2. Do you think game shows today are fair?
3. Are the players today special people (like Van Doren)? Or are they ordinary people (like Herbert Stempel). Give examples.

# STUDENT ACTIVITIES

## UNIT 1 ◆ A WORLD OF FRIENDS, A WORLD OF PEACE

SECTION 5B, EXERCISE 1, PAGE 11

**①** **A.** *Student B, you are Adam. You are talking to your father on the phone. Listen carefully to the questions. Choose sentence **a** or **b** to answer the questions. Only one answer makes sense.*

1. **a.** I'm in Ukraine.
   **b.** I'm having a great time.
2. **a.** It was great. I wanted to spend another week there.
   **b.** It's great. I'm going sightseeing all around.
3. **a.** Yes, they're nice! I feel very comfortable with them.
   **b.** They like American sports.
4. **a.** Yeah, they want to learn English.
   **b.** Yeah, they speak a little English.

**B.** *Change roles. You are Adam's father. Ask Adam the questions below. Listen carefully to the answers.*

1. How about their son? Does he speak English?
2. Will he visit us in New Jersey?
3. Do you have many friends?
4. Did you learn a lot about life in Ukraine?

## UNIT 2 ◆ DO YOU LIKE RAP MUSIC?

SECTION 6B, PAGE 35

**A.** *Student B: Listen to Student A's sentences. Ask for definitions of the following words.*

1. graffiti
2. break dancing
3. rapper
4. rhyme

**Example**

STUDENT A: Hip-hop artists put graffiti on buildings and trains in New York City.

STUDENT B: What is *graffiti*?

STUDENT A: *Graffiti* is hop-hop art. It is writing on buildings and other public places.

*(continued on next page)*

159

*B. Change roles. Read sentences 1 to 4. one at a time. Student A will ask for definitions. Look at the box below. Give the definitions of the words Student B asks about.*

1. The DJ at the party was great! We danced all night.

2. There are many nonsense words in rap songs.

3. A lot of people think that gangsta rap is bad.

4. Many rappers use drum machines to make their music.

---

**Definitions**

A **DJ** is a person who plays music on the radio or at parties.

**Nonsense words** are words with no meaning.

**Gangsta rap** is rap music about violence.

**Drum machines** are electronic machines that make music.

---

## UNIT 3 ◆ DIAMONDS ARE FOREVER

SECTION 5A, EXERCISE 2, PAGE 45

**2** *Student B, answer your partner's questions about your pictures. Then ask your partner these yes/no questions about his or her pictures. Remember to use rising intonation.*

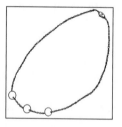

1. Do you see a pearl necklace?

2. Does it have three pearls?

3. Are the pearls small?

4. Do you see a diamond ring?

5. _____ ?
   (Your question)

6. _____ ?
   (Your question)

## UNIT 4 ◆ MEMORIES: LOST AND FOUND

SECTION 5B, EXERCISE 1, PAGE 63

**1** *Student B, listen to Student A. Choose the correct response.*

a. That's great. I'm sure that life is very difficult when a relative has Alzheimer's disease.

b. That's sad, but maybe she can become a member of a support group. You can write to the Alzheimer's Association for more information.

c. I know, but if they join a group, they usually feel better about themselves.

d. Don't worry, that's normal! Everybody forgets things sometimes.

*Change roles. Read the sentences. Listen to your partner's response. Does it make sense? If it doesn't make sense, tell your partner, "I don't think that's right."*

5. In the writer's group, the psychologist is not the only person who helps the members.

6. In support groups, the members often become good friends.

7. When Elsa got Alzheimer's disease, she couldn't keep her job as a nurse.

8. I can't remember anything that happened before I was four years old. Can you?

## UNIT 6 ◆ FROM SADNESS TO STRENGTH

SECTION 6B, PAGE 108

*Student B, listen to Student A's statements. Ask for an example. Use the questions below:*

Could you give me an example?

Can you give me an example?

Like what, for example?

Like what?

*(continued on next page)*

*Change roles. Read each general statement about Eleanor Roosevelt out loud. Student A will ask for an example. Choose the correct example from the list below. Read it to Student A.*

## General Statements

**4.** Jane Barlow's book gives a lot of new information about Eleanor Roosevelt.

**5.** When FDR was president, Eleanor really wanted to be independent, so she took some jobs to earn money.

**6.** People sometimes said bad things about Eleanor.

## Examples

**d.** Some people said she was ugly. Other people said she was too independent. They said that a first lady shouldn't work.

**e.** She wrote for a newspaper and had a radio show, and she even did some advertisements!

**f.** Well, she explains that when Eleanor got older, she really had a happy personal life, and a lot of good friends. Other books said she was an unhappy and lonely adult.

## UNIT 7 ◆ DRIVING YOU CRAZY

SECTION 5A, EXERCISE 2, PAGE 120

**2** *Student B, listen to Student A. Write the number of syllables in each word.*

1. ____
2. ____
3. ____
4. ____
5. ____

*Change roles. Say each word below.*

6. honk

7. accident

8. crowded

9. injured

10. tailgated

# THE PHONETIC ALPHABET

## Consonant Symbols

| | | | |
|---|---|---|---|
| /b/ | be | /t/ | to |
| /d/ | do | /v/ | van |
| /f/ | father | /w/ | will |
| /g/ | get | /y/ | yes |
| /h/ | he | /z/ | zoo, busy |
| /k/ | keep, can | /θ/ | thanks |
| /l/ | let | /ð/ | then |
| /m/ | may | /ʃ/ | she |
| /n/ | no | /ʒ/ | vision, Asia |
| /p/ | pen | /tʃ/ | child |
| /r/ | rain | /dʒ/ | join |
| /s/ | so, circle | /ŋ/ | long |

## Vowel Symbols

| | | | |
|---|---|---|---|
| /ɑ/ | far, hot | /iy/ | we, mean, feet |
| /ɛ/ | met, said | /ey/ | day, late, rain |
| /ɔ/ | tall, bought | /ow/ | go, low, coat |
| /ə/ | son, under | /uw/ | too, blue |
| /æ/ | cat | /ay/ | time, buy |
| /ɪ/ | ship | /aw/ | house, now |
| /ʊ/ | good, could, put | /oy/ | boy, coin |

## UNIT 1 ◆ A WORLD OF FRIENDS, A WORLD OF PEACE

### 3. LISTENING ONE: "Hello. This is the Friendship Force."

**3A.** *Introducing the Topic*

**Recording:** Hello. This is the Friendship Force. The Friendship Force helps people make friends all over the world because "A world of friends is a world of peace." For more information about the Friendship Force, press 1. To speak with someone about Friendship Force groups, press 2.

**Rick:** Hello, Friendship Force. Rick speaking.

**Nina:** Hi, I have some questions about the Friendship Force.

**3B.** *Listening for Main Ideas*

**Recording:** Hello. This is the Friendship Force. The Friendship Force helps people make friends all over the world because "A world of friends is a world of peace." For more information about the Friendship Force, press 1. To speak with someone about Friendship Force groups, press 2.

**Rick:** Hello, Friendship Force. Rick speaking.

**Nina:** Hi, I have some questions about the Friendship Force.

**Rick:** Sure, what would you like to know?

**Nina:** Well, can you tell me . . . can college students join?

**Rick:** Sure. There are lots of students in the Friendship Force.

**Nina:** Oh, good.

**Rick:** But you know, the Friendship Force isn't for everyone. Friendship Force visitors live in a family's home, not a hotel. Some people aren't comfortable living with a family in a different culture for two weeks.

**Nina:** Oh, I understand. That's no problem for me.

**Rick:** Great!

**Nina:** But what about language? I only speak English.

**Rick:** That isn't a problem. Some host families speak other languages, and some don't. But Friendship Force visitors and their host families always become good friends.

**Nina:** That's good! Ummm . . . I have another question. Do the visitors have any time to travel?

**Rick:** Sure. Most visitors spend two weeks with their host family, and after that they travel around the country. But you know, we think making new friends is more important than

**Nina:** I like that!

**Rick:** Good. Do you have any other questions?

**Nina:** Um . . . Yes . . . What about the cost?

**Rick:** You pay for two things: your plane ticket, and a hundred dollars to join the Friendship Force.

**Nina:** OK, great! Could you send me an application?

**Rick:** Sure! What's your name?

**Nina:** It's Nina, N-I-N-A, Rodriguez, R-O-D-R-I-G-U-E-Z.

**Rick:** OK, and your address?

**Nina:** It's 12 Northfield Road. Cleveland, Ohio. 44146.

**Rick:** OK, 12—Northfield Road—Cleveland—44146.

**Nina:** Right.

**Rick:** OK, then. Great. I'll send the application right away.

**Nina:** Thanks so much.

**Rick:** You're welcome. Good luck.

**Nina:** Bye.

**3C.** *Listening for Details*
(repeat Section 3B)

**3D.** *Listening between the Lines*

**Excerpt 1**

**Rick:** But you know, the Friendship Force isn't for everyone. Friendship Force visitors live in a family's home, not a hotel. Some people aren't comfortable living with a family in a different culture for two weeks.

**Nina:** Oh, I understand. That's no problem for me.

**Rick:** Great!

**Excerpt 2**

**Nina:** But what about language? I only speak English.

**Rick:** That isn't a problem.

**Excerpt 3**

**Rick:** But you know, we think making new friends is more important than sightseeing. We say, "People, not places."

**Nina:** I like that!

## 4. LISTENING TWO: The Best Time in My Life

### 4A. *Expanding the Topic*

**Adam:** Hi. I'm Adam Marchuk. I was a Friendship Force visitor in Ukraine when I was in high school. What was it like? Well, it was great. Actually, it was amazing. The Friendship Force is not like taking a trip. I mean, you live with a host family. You eat breakfast with them, you see where they work and go to school, you watch TV with them, you go out with them on the weekends.

I became really good friends with my host family, especially my host brother Vadim. You know . . . it's amazing, you don't really need to speak the same language to be friends. I mean . . . if you want to communicate, you just start talking.

Last year, Vadim, came to visit my family in New Jersey. We had a great time and we went to a lot of basketball games! His English is better now, but my Ukrainian is still pretty bad!

Anyway, we e-mail each other all the time. Vadim tells me about the family, about his university. Now, he also asks me about basketball. He loves the U.S. players.

You know, The Friendship Force really changed my life. I learned so much—about Ukranian people and their culture. I also learned a lot about myself. You know, you *can't* learn those things from sightseeing. I'm more interested in the world now. Now I want to work for world peace.

## 5. REVIEWING LANGUAGE

### 5A. *Exploring Language: Letters of the Alphabet*
**1** 1. A B C D E F G H I J K L M N O P Q
R S T U V W X Y Z
**2** 2. A E I O U

## UNIT 2 ◆ DO YOU LIKE RAP MUSIC?

## 1. APPROACHING THE TOPIC

### 1B. *Sharing Information*
*Rapper's Delight* (Sugarhill Gang, 1979)
I said a hip <u>hop</u>
The hippie to the hippie
The hip hip a hop, and <u>you don't stop</u>, a <u>rock it</u>

To the bang bang <u>boogie</u>, say <u>up jump</u> the boogie,
To <u>the rhythm of the boogie,</u> <u>the beat.</u>
A skiddleebebop, we rock, scooby doo,
And guess what America, we love you.

## 3. LISTENING ONE: A Famous Rapper: Tupac Shakur

### 3A. *Introducing the Topic*
**Eli Jones:** This is Eli Jones on WKRZ. Tonight, my guest is the famous rap musician, King Kool.

**King Kool:** Hi Eli. It's nice to be here.

**Eli Jones:** Welcome King Kool. This evening, we're talking about the great rapper, Tupac Shakur, and we're taking calls from listeners. King Kool, you knew Tupac. Can you tell us about his life?

### 3B. *Listening for Main Ideas*
**Eli Jones:** This is Eli Jones on WKRZ. Tonight, my guest is the famous rap musician, King Kool.

**King Kool:** Hi Eli. It's nice to be here.

**Eli Jones:** Welcome King Kool. This evening, we're talking about the great rapper, Tupac Shakur, and we're taking calls from listeners. King Kool, you knew Tupac. Can you tell us about his life?

**King Kool:** Well, his life was too short . . . and it was difficult. He wasn't a happy child.

**Eli Jones:** Really . . .

**King Kool:** Mmhmm. His family was poor; and he never knew his father. . . .

**Eli Jones:** What about his mother?

**King Kool:** Oh, she loved Tupac. She called Tupac "the Black Prince."

**Eli Jones:** The Black Prince? *What does that mean?*

**King Kool:** Well, she always said, "Tupac is going to be an important man for African Americans." And he was.

**Eli Jones:** OK . . . We have our first call . . . Hello?

**King Kool:** Hi!

**Eli Jones:** Hi! Do you have a question for King Kool?

**Caller 1:** Yes. My question is: When did Tupac get interested in rap?

**King Kool:** Well, I know he started writing rap songs when he was 15.

**Caller 1:** Wow . . .

**King Kool:** Yeah . . . and when he wrote songs, he started to feel good, to feel happy. He really loved writing songs. And his songs were about his life.

**Eli Jones:** Yeah . . . His songs were serious.

**King Kool:** That's right. They were different from other rap songs. The words in his songs also had really interesting rhymes, and his music had a fantastic rhythm, too.

**Eli Jones:** Yeah, Tupac's music became popular very quickly! I think to young African Americans, Tupac Shakur was the best.

**King Kool:** Yeah, they felt that he really understood them. His songs told about *their* lives too.

**Eli Jones:** We have another call. Hello!

**Caller 2:** How can you say that Tupac's music is great?! He wrote "gangsta rap." His songs are about violence!

**Eli Jones:** King Kool, please tell our listeners . . . What *is* "gangsta rap?"

**King Kool:** "Gangsta rap" is the name for rap songs about guns and violence . . . And the caller is right . . . Tupac wrote about violence, because violence was part of his life. . . .

**Eli Jones:** uh-huh . . .

**King Kool:** He had a lot of problems with the police . . .

**Caller 2:** That's right! He did.

**King Kool:** . . . but Tupac didn't say that violence was good! He just wanted people to know what was happening.

**Eli Jones:** His life ended in violence too.

**King Kool:** Yes. Tupac always said "I'm going to die young." He knew it. But his music will live forever. That's for sure.

**Eli Jones:** Well, we're out of time for tonight. King Kool, thanks for speaking with us.

**King Kool:** My pleasure.

**3C.** *Listening for Details*
(repeat Section 3B)

**3D.** *Listening between the Lines*

**Excerpt 1**
**King Kool:** Well, I know he started writing rap songs when he was 15.

**Caller 1:** Wow . . .

**King Kool:** Yeah . . . and when he wrote songs, he started to feel good, to feel happy. He really loved writing songs. And his songs were about his life.

**Eli Jones:** Yeah . . . His songs were serious.

**Excerpt 2**
**Eli Jones:** Yeah, Tupac's music became popular very quickly! I think to young African Americans, Tupac Shakur was the best.

**King Kool:** Yeah, they felt that he really understood them. His songs told about their lives too.

**Excerpt 3**
**Caller 2:** How can you say that Tupac's music is great?! He wrote "gangsta rap." His songs are about violence!

**4. LISTENING TWO: A Rap Song**

**4A.** *Expanding the Topic*
*Keep Ya Head Up* (Tupac Shakur, 1993)

Last night my buddy lost his whole family
It's gonna take the man in me to conquer this insanity
It seems the rain'll never let up
I try to keep my head up, and still keep from gettin' wet up
You know it's funny,
when it rains, it pours
They got money for wars, but can't feed the poor
Say there ain't no hope for the youth
And the truth is
It ain't no hope for the future

**5. REVIEWING LANGUAGE**

**5A.** *Exploring Language: Pronunciation of /æ/*

①  and       can       sad       an       fantastic
    rap       family       that       had       thanks

②  At first, hip-hop was music, dance and art. Later, hip-hop began to have its own fashion, or clothing style too. Rap musicians wore very big pants and T-shirts. On their heads, they wore matching wool hats. Or they wore baseball caps, turned backward. They liked clothes made by famous designers, like Tommy Hilfiger. They liked expensive sports shoes and gold jewelry. Hip-hop fashion became very popular. Soon young people all over the United States had clothes like rappers.

**UNIT 3 ◆ DIAMONDS ARE FOREVER**

**3. LISTENING ONE: The Hope Diamond**

**3A.** *Introducing the Topic*

**Tour Guide:** Here we are—the Hope Diamond. Millions of people come to see this diamond every year. It's the most valuable diamond in the world.

**Katelyn:** How much is it worth?

**Tour Guide:** The Hope Diamond is worth 250 million dollars.

**Crowd:** Wow

**Tour Guide:** Yes, it's the most valuable diamond in the world, but that's not all. This diamond has a fascinating history.

### 3B. *Listening for Main Ideas*

**Tour Guide:** Here we are—the Hope Diamond. Millions of people come to see this diamond every year. It's the most valuable diamond in the world.

**Katelyn:** How much is it worth?

**Tour Guide:** The Hope Diamond is worth 250 million dollars.

**Crowd:** Wow

**Tour Guide:** Yes, it's the most valuable diamond in the world, but that's not all. This diamond has a fascinating history.

**Bob:** Is this the diamond that what's-his-name bought for what's-her-name? You know—the famous movie star's diamond?

**Tour Guide:** No. King Louis the XIV of France owned this diamond. Imagine . . . it's 1668 and you are Louis the XIV. A man comes to you from India with a huge blue diamond. It weighs 112 carats! You buy it from him and your jeweler cuts it so it's very beautiful and it sparkles. Now it weighs 67 carats, and this beautiful jewel is called the "Blue Diamond of the Crown" . . .

**Katelyn:** Oh, I think I know the rest of the story. Somebody steals it, right?

**Tour Guide:** Yes. In 1792, somebody steals it and it is gone for a long, long time. Then it appears in London, but it's cut down to 44 carats. It's smaller, but it still has that beautiful clear blue color. Then a wealthy man buys it. His name is Henry Philip Hope, and that's why we call it the Hope Diamond.

**Katelyn:** Oh, so the name doesn't mean "hope" or "good luck" or anything like that?

**Tour Guide:** Not at all. Listen to the rest of the story. A wealthy American woman buys it, and then she has some very bad luck.

**Katelyn:** What happens?

**Tour Guide:** Well, first her son dies in a car accident, and then her daughter kills herself. And finally—her husband goes crazy!

**Bob:** That's not because of a diamond! How can a diamond bring bad luck?

**Tour Guide:** Well, actually, some people think that . . .

### 3C. *Listening for Details*
(repeat Section 3B)

### 3D. *Listening between the Lines*

**Excerpt 1**

**Bob:** Is this the diamond that what's-his-name bought for what's-her-name? You know—the famous movie star's diamond?

**Excerpt 2**

**Katelyn:** Oh, so the name doesn't mean "hope" or "good luck" or anything like that?

**Excerpt 3**

**Bob:** That's not because of a diamond! How can a diamond bring bad luck?

## 4. LISTENING TWO: Shopping for Diamonds

### 4A. *Expanding the Topic*

**Bob:** Hey, look, Katelyn, it's a jewelry store. Why don't we go in and look at rings?

**Katelyn:** What kind of rings?

**Bob:** Uh, I don't know. How about engagement rings?

**Katelyn:** Bob, are you proposing? Right here?

**Bob:** Yes. I'm proposing. I love you. I want to marry you. Will you marry me? Will you be my wife?

**Katelyn:** Finally! Yes!

**Saleswoman:** May I help you?

**Bob:** Uh, yes. We want to look at some rings . . . Do you have any . . . uh, engagement rings?

**Saleswoman:** Yes, of course. Are you interested in diamond rings?

**Katelyn:** Well, sure. Let's look at the diamonds.

**Saleswoman:** The diamonds are right over here Is this your first diamond?

**Bob:** Yes.

**Saleswoman:** Well, then, I'd like to tell you about the Four Cs. The Four Cs help you to choose a diamond. The first C is cut. With the right cut, a diamond really sparkles. Look.

**Katelyn and Bob:** Wow.

**Saleswoman:** The second C is color. Most valuable diamonds have no color at all. Of course, the Hope diamond is blue, but *most* valuable diamonds have *no* color. The third C is clarity. You see, an excellent diamond is very, very clear. Now the fourth C is also important. It's . . .

**Bob:** Let me guess. "*Cash*," right? You need a lot of money to buy a diamond.

**Saleswoman:** Well, no, actually, the fourth C is carat. Carat means how much the diamond weighs. And, yes, it's true that a heavier diamond is more valuable. Now what kind of diamond would you like to see? How large?

**Katelyn:** Very large! Very, very large.

**Bob:** Oh, please don't listen to her. Let's take a look at . . . a medium size . . . Yeah. How about starting with that one?

## 5. REVIEWING LANGUAGE

**5A.** *Exploring Language: Rising Intonation*
1. Are you interested in diamond rings?
2. Is this your first diamond?
3. Do you have cash?

## UNIT 4 ◆ MEMORIES LOST AND FOUND

## 3. LISTENING ONE: I Remember

### 3A. *Introducing the Topic*

**Jane Oliver:** Good evening. Welcome to the Alzheimer's Family Meeting. Tonight, our speaker is Dr. Alan Dienstag. Dr. Dienstag is a psychologist, and he has started a new group for people with Alzheimer's disease. It's a writers' group, and I think some of your relatives may be interested in it. Please feel free to ask him questions. Dr. Dienstag, welcome.

### 3B. *Listening for Main Ideas*

**Jane Oliver:** Good evening. Welcome to the Alzheimer's Family Meeting. Tonight, our speaker is Dr. Alan Dienstag. Dr. Dienstag is a psychologist, and he has started a new group for people with Alzheimer's disease. It's a writers' group, and I think some of your relatives may be interested in it. Please feel free to ask him questions. Dr. Dienstag, welcome.

**Dr. Dienstag:** Thank you, Ms. Oliver. Hello, everyone. Yes, my group *is* a writers' group, and it *is* for people with Alzheimer's. The members meet once a week, and they write stories about their past. Then they read their stories to the group, and we all talk about them.

**Relative 1:** Excuse me, but my father sometimes doesn't remember my name! How can writing a story help him?

**Dr. Dienstag:** Well, people with Alzheimer's forget so many things. But they often remember the past very well. When they can remember something and can write a story about it, they feel better about themselves.

**Relative 1:** Well, OK, but why do they meet in a group?

**Dr. Dienstag:** Well, because, as you know, people with Alzheimer's often forget words. So, they can't always explain their ideas. But when they meet in a group, they can help each other.

**Relative 1:** Really?

**Dr. Dienstag:** Yes, it's amazing. Together, they find the right words to explain their ideas. And then they all feel better about themselves.

**Relative 2:** I think that's wonderful. And it's a nice way to make new friends, too.

**Dr. Dienstag:** Yes, and that's very important. As you know, many people with Alzheimer's lose their old friends. They feel lonely. But in the writers' group, they can talk about their feelings. By talking together and writing together, the members become good friends. They really understand each other.

**Relative 2:** What do they write about?

**Dr. Dienstag:** Well, every week, they write about a different memory. But they always begin with the same two words: "I remember."

**Relative 3:** That's interesting. We usually think about the things they *don't* remember.

**Dr. Dienstag:** That's very true. You know, Alzheimer's is a terrible disease. My group members know this too. But every week, they are so happy to get together to write and talk and laugh.

**Jane Oliver:** Thank you, Dr. Dienstag.

### 3C. *Listening for Details*
(repeat Section 3B)

### 3D. *Listening between the Lines*

**Excerpt 1**

**Relative 1:** Excuse me, but my father sometimes doesn't remember my name! How can writing a story help him?

**Excerpt 2**

**Dr. Dienstag:** Well, people with Alzheimer's forget so many things. But they often remember the past very well. When they can remember something and can write a story about it, they feel better about themselves.

**Excerpt 3**

**Dr. Dienstag:** Together, they find the right words to explain their ideas. And then they all feel better about themselves.

**Relative 2:** I think that's wonderful. And it's a nice way to make new friends, too.

## 4. LISTENING TWO: Elsa's Story

**4A.** *Expanding the Topic*

**Elsa:** I remember I was four or five years old, and I looked up and I saw the sky and it looked like an ocean with waves, and my mother told me that it was called . . . oh . . . it has a special name . . . The clouds had all these waves, wavy lines . . . ummm . . . Oh dear . . . I can't remember this word . . .

**Dr. Dienstag:** Is it the nighttime sky or the daytime sky?

**Elsa:** It's a nice time, I mean, nighttime.

**Sam:** Is it a star?

**Elsa:** No, it's . . . it has a name . . . it's a fish . . .

**Sarah:** Mackerel sky!

**Elsa:** Ah! Mackerel sky!

**Dr. Dienstag:** A mackerel sky, you mean when the clouds look like the waves on the back of a fish—a mackerel. OK Elsa, you can go on with your story now.

## 5. REVIEWING LANGUAGE

**5A.** *Exploring Language: Pronunciation of /eɪ/ and /ɛ/*

**(1)** may   name   waves   they   always
yes   forget   remember   help   many

**(2)**
1. welcome
2. member
3. same
4. better
5. daytime
6. together
7. make
8. friends

**(3) Jane Oliver:** Dr. Dienstag, I have a question too. How did you get the idea for an Alzheimer's writers' group?

**Dr. Dienstag:**
1. Well, I have to say, it really wasn't my idea!
2. The idea came from a famous writer named Don DeLillo.
3. His mother-in-law had Alzheimer's, and I met her.
4. She wanted to remember things.
5. But she was forgetting more and more every day
6. Don DeLillo was looking for a way to help his mother-in-law.
7. One day, he told me his idea about a writers' group.
8. I thought it was a great idea.
9. So we decided to work together.

## UNIT 5 ◆ THINKING YOUNG: CREATIVITY IN BUSINESS

### 3. LISTENING ONE: K-K Gregory, Young and Creative

**3A.** *Introducing the Topic*

**Professor Ray:** Today we have a guest speaker, K-K Gregory. She's a successful business owner, and she's only seventeen. Her company makes Wristies.

**K-K Gregory:** Thank you, Professor Ray . . . Hi, . . . umm . . . I'm really excited to be here. Actually, I started my company when I was ten.

**3B.** *Listening for Main Ideas*

**Professor Ray:** Today we have a guest speaker, K-K Gregory. She's a successful business owner, and she's only seventeen. Her company makes Wristies.

**K-K Gregory:** Thank you, Professor Ray . . . Hi, . . . umm . . . I'm really excited to be here. Actually, I started my company when I was ten. Really! . . . it's true! These are Wristies. See . . . they're long *gloves* with no *fingers*. They keep your *wrists* warm and dry, but your fingers can move easily. So, you can wear them outside, for sports or . . . um . . . work. But you can also wear them inside, in a cold house or office.

**Professor Ray:** Ah, K-K, tell us how you got the idea for Wristies.

**K-K Gregory:** Well, it was winter, and there was a lot of snow, and I was playing in it. I was wearing a jacket and gloves, but my wrists were really cold! That's when I got the idea. I just thought of it. So I went home and first, I looked for some warm material. Then I put it around each arm. And then I made a little hole for my thumb. And that's how I made the first pair of Wristies.

**Professor Ray:** Great! Are there any questions?

**Student 1:** Yes. So, how did you decide to start a business?

**K-K Gregory:** Well, at first, I didn't think about starting a business at all. I just made Wristies for my friends, in different colors, and they all loved them. It was really great! Then they said, "You know, you can sell these things!" And my mother helped me to start my company.

**K-K Gregory:** Did she have any business experience?

**K-K Gregory:**   No! My mother didn't know anything about business, and I didn't either. But we talked to a lot of people and asked a lot of questions, and, ya know, we learned a lot! And we had fun . . . Yeah?

**Student 3:**   Where can you buy Wristies?

**K-K Gregory:**   In stores. You can buy them in a lot of stores, and there's also a website. Once I went on a TV shopping show, and I sold a thousand pairs of Wristies in one hour! I couldn't believe it . . .

**Students:**   Wow!

**K-K Gregory:**   Yeah, it was exciting!

**Professor Ray:**   We only have a few more minutes. Is there one more question? Yes?

**Student 4:**   K-K, do you have any advice for us?

**K-K Gregory:**   Well, umm . . . Listen to your friends. And, be creative. And . . . don't be afraid to do something new.

**3C.** *Listening for Details*
(repeat Section 3B)

**3D.** *Listening between the Lines*

**Excerpt 1**

**K-K Gregory:**   Actually, I started my company when I was ten. Really! . . . it's true!

**Excerpt 2**

**K-K Gregory:**   My mother didn't know anything about business, and I didn't either. But we talked to a lot of people and asked a lot of questions, and, ya know, we learned a lot! And we had fun

**Excerpt 3**

**K-K Gregory:**   Once I went on a TV shopping show, and I sold a thousand pairs of Wristies in one hour! I couldn't believe it . . .

**Students:**   Wow!

**K-K Gregory:**   Yeah, it was exciting!

## 4. LISTENING TWO: A Business Class

**4A.** *Expanding the Topic*

**①** **Professor Ray:**   OK, so what can we learn from K-K? . . . First of all, she made something that she needed. She had a creative idea—to make Wristies. Then, she really listened to other people. Her friends liked Wristies. They liked them a lot. Her mother liked them, too. Finally, she decided to make Wristies into a business. She didn't know anything about business, but she wasn't afraid. The point is: Children *think* they can do *any*thing—and sometimes they *can*—because they

aren't afraid! *Our* problem is—we're not children anymore! We *are* afraid, we're nervous, people tell us, "Don't make mistakes!" So we *stop* being creative . . . But we *can learn* to be creative again *if* we can remember the feeling of being a child. And this is how to do it:

OK, first, close your eyes . . . Relax . . . relax. Remember when you were a child . . . Think about a time you did something new, and you weren't afraid . . . you weren't nervous. . . . You did it . . . and you felt good . . . Take your time . . . Then, open your eyes and tell your story to another student. And then we'll discuss your stories.

**②** **Professor Ray:**   But we *can learn* to be creative again *if* we can remember the feeling of being a child.  And this is how to do it:

OK, first, close your eyes . . . Relax . . . relax. Remember when you were a child . . . Think about a time you did something new, and you weren't afraid . . . you weren't nervous. . . . You did it . . . and you felt good . . . Take your time . . . Then, open your eyes and tell your story to another student. And then we'll discuss your stories.

## 5. REVIEWING LANGUAGE

**5A.** *Exploring Language: Pronunciation of* "th"

**①** they   there   that's   mother   breathe
thanks   thought   things   anything   with

**②** 1. They're long gloves with no fingers.
2. There's a hole for the thumb.
3. Some people wear them outside; others wear them inside.
4. So then I thought, " I can sell these things!"
5. My mother didn't know anything about business.
6. You can buy them in stores and there's also a website.

## UNIT 6 ◆ FROM SADNESS TO STRENGTH

## 3. LISTENING ONE: A Very Unusual Woman, Part 1

**3A.** *Introducing the Topic*

**Henry Samuels:**   Welcome to *Booktalk*. Today we're talking to Jane Barlow. She just wrote a new book about Eleanor Roosevelt. Professor Barlow, why was Eleanor Roosevelt such an important woman in U.S. history?

**Jane Barlow:**   Well, she was a very unusual woman. In her time, she did things that most women didn't do.

**3B.** *Listening for Main Ideas*

**Henry Samuels:** Welcome to *Booktalk*. Today we're talking to Jane Barlow. She just wrote a new book about Eleanor Roosevelt. Professor Barlow, why was Eleanor Roosevelt such an important woman in U.S. history?

**Jane Barlow:** Well, she was a very unusual woman. In her time, she did things that most women didn't do.

**Henry Samuels:** Like what, for example?

**Jane Barlow:** Well, she worked in politics. When her husband was governor of New York, he became sick and he couldn't walk. So Eleanor did some of his work.

**Henry Samuels:** She traveled a lot for him, didn't she?

**Jane Barlow:** Yes, she traveled all around New York and made political speeches for her husband. And she really enjoyed it.

**Henry Samuels:** And what did people in New York think of her then?

**Jane Barlow:** Oh, they loved her! So then, in 1933, when FDR, became president of the United States, Eleanor was already popular. She became a new kind of first lady.

**Henry Samuels:** What do you mean?

**Jane Barlow:** Well, most first ladies weren't very independent. But Eleanor wanted to be different. She had her own ideas, and she wanted to speak out about them.

**Henry Samuels:** What kind of ideas? Could you give us an example?

**Jane Barlow:** Sure. Eleanor wanted every person to go to school and have a good job. She especially wanted to help women, children, and poor people.

**Henry Samuels:** Mmmhmm.

**Jane Barlow:** And she wanted peace in the world. So she spoke out about her ideas. She wrote in the newspaper; she spoke on the radio; and she traveled all over the world.

**Henry Samuels:** I know people everywhere respected her . . .

**Jane Barlow:** Yes. She was so strong and independent, and she really wanted to help people. But some people didn't *like* her!

**Henry Samuels:** Really?

**Jane Barlow:** Look, Eleanor was not a traditional woman. Some people said she was *too* strong and independent. They even said she was ugly!

**Henry Samuels:** *Really?!* How did Eleanor feel when she heard those things?

**Jane Barlow:** Well, Eleanor Roosevelt *was* a strong woman. So she just laughed.

**Henry Samuels:** Thank you, Professor. We'll be back with more in just a minute.

**3C.** *Listening for Details*
(repeat Section 3B)

**3D.** *Listening between the Lines*

**Excerpt 1**

**Jane Barlow:** Well, she worked in politics. When her husband was governor of New York, he became sick and he couldn't walk. So Eleanor did some of his work.

**Henry Samuels:** She traveled a lot for him, didn't she?

**Jane Barlow:** Yes, she traveled all around New York and made political speeches for her husband. And she really enjoyed it.

**Henry Samuels:** And what did people in New York think of her then?

**Jane Barlow:** Oh, they loved her! So then, in 1933, when FDR, became president of the United States, Eleanor was already popular. She became a new kind of first lady.

**Excerpt 2**

**Jane Barlow:** Eleanor wanted every person to go to school and have a good job. She especially wanted to help women, children, and poor people.

**Henry Samuels:** Mmmhmm.

**Jane Barlow:** And she wanted peace in the world. So she spoke out about her ideas. She wrote in the newspaper; she spoke on the radio; and she traveled all over the world.

**Excerpt 3**

**Jane Barlow:** But some people didn't like her!

**Henry Samuels:** Really?

**Jane Barlow:** Look, Eleanor was not a traditional woman. Some people said she was too strong and independent. They even said she was ugly!

**Henry Samuels:** *Really?!* How did Eleanor feel when she heard those things?

**Jane Barlow:** Well, Eleanor Roosevelt *was* a strong woman. So she just laughed.

**4. LISTENING TWO: A Very Unusual Woman, Part 2**

**4A.** *Expanding the Topic*

**Henry Samuels:** Welcome back to *Booktalk*. Professor Barlow, there are so many books about Eleanor Roosevelt. Why did you want to write one too?

**Jane Barlow:** Well, I felt that most writers—especially men—didn't really understand Eleanor's life. I wanted to give a woman's point of view.

**Henry Samuels:** What do you mean?

**Jane Barlow:** Well, for example, everybody knows that FDR was not a good husband. So, many writers said that Eleanor was unhappy all her life.

**Henry Samuels:** And what do you think?

**Jane Barlow:** I think that's not true! I mean, of course Eleanor was unhappy for a while . . . Her husband didn't love her anymore! And she was very angry. For two years she couldn't eat or sleep well. But, as time passed, Eleanor's feelings changed. She stopped feeling angry.

**Henry Samuels:** Really?

**Jane Barlow:** Yes. Eleanor saw that a good marriage wasn't the only way for her to be happy. She remembered the important lessons that she learned from her teacher, Marie Souvestre . . .

**Henry Samuels:** Mmmhmm . . .

**Jane Barlow:** . . . and she decided to have an independent life.

**Henry Samuels:** How did she do that?

**Jane Barlow:** Well, Eleanor had her work. It was important, and she loved it. But she also had many good friends, both women *and* men. Her work and her friendships made her life very happy.

**Henry Samuels:** Professor Jane Barlow, thank you for talking with us today.

**Jane Barlow:** Thank you, Henry.

## 5. REVIEWING LANGUAGE

### 5A. *Exploring Language: Pronunciation of* -ed *endings*

**1** 1. liked
2. died
3. explained
4. helped
5. believed
6. worked
7. wanted
8. married
9. respected

**2** 1. As time passed, Eleanor realized that she didn't want to be sad forever.
2. She decided that she could have a happy, independent life.
3. She wanted to do important work.
4. Eleanor knew that people listened to her when she talked.
5. Eleanor knew that many people in the world needed help.
6. So she traveled around the world and tried to help people.

7. She visited so many countries that people called her "The First Lady of the World."
8. People around the world loved and respected Eleanor Roosevelt.

## UNIT 7 ◆ DRIVING YOU CRAZY

### 3. LISTENING ONE: Road Rage

### 3A. *Introducing the Topic*

**Instructor:** Good evening, class. Welcome to Traffic School. Tonight we have two speakers, John and Marie. They have true stories about road rage—something we hear a lot about today. Road rage means getting angry at other drivers. Sometimes it's simple. One driver honks the horn at another driver or tries to move ahead of him. But road rage can also be very dangerous. Do you know how many people are killed in the United States because of road rage? More than 200 people every year. And 12,000 more are injured. This is one of the most serious driving problems.

### 3B. *Listening for Main Ideas*

**Instructor:** Good evening, class. Welcome to Traffic School. Tonight we have two speakers, John and Marie. They have true stories about road rage—something we hear a lot about today. Road rage means getting angry at other drivers. Sometimes it's simple. One driver honks the horn at another driver or tries to move ahead of him. But road rage can also be very dangerous. Do you know how many people are killed in the United States because of road rage? More than 200 people every year. And 12,000 more are injured. This is one of the most serious driving problems. Listen to John's story.

**John:** Last year I was driving home from work and I almost got killed. It was late. Do you know how you feel when you're really tired? Well, I changed lanes on the highway and I forgot to use my signal. Suddenly I saw a bright light behind me. This guy in a big truck was right behind me. He was following me. I was scared, so I started going a little faster. He went faster, too. He was coming after me! I got off the highway and drove into the parking lot of a big supermarket. He followed me into the parking lot. I thought he was going to hit my car with his truck. But he didn't. He just drove right past me, yelling at me. Then he left. I was really lucky.

**Instructor:** John *was* lucky. Sometimes people actually try to hit other people with their cars. This driver probably didn't hit John because there were other people in the parking lot. They could see him, so he wasn't anonymous anymore. That's one reason for road rage—people feel anonymous in their cars. Nobody knows who they are. They can do things that they usually don't do. Like Marie, for example. She looks like a very nice person. But listen to what she did last year—before she learned how to control her road rage.

**Marie:** Well, I was driving to work when I saw this man in a red sports car. He was crossing the intersection. I let him go ahead of me and get on the highway first. Usually people wave at you to say "thanks," but he didn't. He just drove away. I don't really know why, but I got very, very angry at him. Why didn't he thank me? I got behind him on the highway and I tailgated him. We were going about 60 miles an hour in heavy traffic, and I stayed right behind him. I knew it was dangerous, but I didn't care. Finally I passed him, driving fast and honking at him. You know what? I still can't believe him! He's the rudest guy on the road! Driving around in his sports car, thinking he's better than other people . . . Ugh! If I ever see him again, I'll—

**Instructor:** Thank you, Marie. In conclusion tonight, I want to tell you that more and more people are driving dangerously. They are stressed out by their jobs and they sometimes have to drive a long way to work. And the roads are more crowded today—70% of the highways in American cities are very, very crowded. More driving, more traffic, more stress—this is why we have road rage. What can you do? You can't control the other driver. You can only control yourself. So, be a safe driver. Be polite. Don't tailgate; don't forget to signal. And if someone makes you angry, forget about it. Turn on the radio; listen to music. Remember: You have only one life to live. Don't lose it to road rage.

### 3C. *Listening for Details*
(repeat Section 3B)

### 3D. *Listening between the Lines*

#### Excerpt 1
**John:** Last year I was driving home from work and I almost got killed. It was late. Do you know how you feel when you're really tired? Well, I changed lanes on the highway and I forgot to use my signal. Suddenly I saw a bright light behind me. This guy in a big truck was right behind me. He was following me. I was scared, so I started going a little faster. He went faster, too. He was coming after me! I got off the highway and drove into the parking lot of a big supermarket. He followed me into the parking lot. I thought he was going to hit my car with his truck.

#### Excerpt 2
**Marie:** Well, I was driving to work when I saw this man in a red sports car. . . . I let him go ahead of me and get on the highway first. Usually people wave at you to say "thanks," but he didn't. He just drove

away. I don't really know why, but I got very, very angry at him . . . Finally I passed him, driving fast and honking at him. . . . Ugh! If I ever see him again . . .

#### Excerpt 3
**Instructor:** In conclusion tonight, I want to tell you that more and more people are driving dangerously. They are stressed out by their jobs and they sometimes have to drive a long way to work. And the roads are more crowded today—70% of the highways in American cities are very, very crowded. More driving, more traffic, more stress—this is why we have road rage. What can you do? You can't control the other driver. You can only control yourself.

## 4. LISTENING TWO: Driving Phobia

### 4A. *Expanding the Topic*
**Psychologist:** Come on, Allen. You can do it. We talked about this. You know what to do.

**Allen:** I know. I know what to do, but I just can't do it.

**Psychologist:** Now what is it, Allen? What exactly are you scared of?

**Allen:** I don't know. I just hate crossing the bridge. I don't want to do it.

**Psychologist:** Come on, Allen. You can do it. Think of all the other things you do: your job, your sports, your music. You're very good at everything you do. You can do this, too.

**Allen:** Too many trucks.

**Psychologist:** What did you say?

**Allen:** I'm scared of the trucks! The trucks are going to hit me!

**Psychologist:** They're not going to hit you, Allen. Don't look at the trucks. The best thing to do is just look at the road.

**Allen:** I can't. There's too much water! What if we fall?

**Psychologist:** Don't think of the water, Allen. Just look at the road. Look straight ahead.

**Allen:** Oh no, we're on the bridge!

**Psychologist:** Keep looking at the road, Allen. Look straight ahead. You're doing fine. Keep going. You're doing fine. There! You did it! You crossed the bridge!

**Allen:** *We* crossed the bridge. I can't do it alone.

**Psychologist:** You will, Allen. You will. Now keep going . . .

## 5. REVIEWING LANGUAGE

### 5A. *Exploring Language, Syllables*

honk
tailgate
dangerous

**1** 1. rage      4. anonymous
2. angry      5. phobia
3. story      6. intersection

## UNIT 8 ◆ ONLY CHILD—LONELY CHILD

### 3. LISTENING ONE: Changing Families

#### 3A. *Introducing the Topic*

**Maria Sanchez:** Hello! Welcome to "Changing Families." I'm Maria Sanchez, and today we're going to talk about only children. In the past, people thought that an only child was sad and lonely. But now, more and more American families are deciding to have just one child, especially in big cities. Today, we are going to meet two families with only children. First, we're going to talk with Marion and Mark Gold, from Chicago, Illinois. Hello!

#### 3B. *Listening for Main Ideas*

**Maria Sanchez:** Hello! Welcome to "Changing Families." I'm Maria Sanchez, and today we're going to talk about only children. In the past, people thought that an only child was sad and lonely. But now, more and more American families are deciding to have just one child, especially in big cities. Today, we are going to meet two families with only children. First, we're going to talk with Marion and Mark Gold, from Chicago, Illinois. Hello!

**Mark and Marion:** Hi Maria.

**Maria:** Welcome! Tell us—Why did you decide to have just one child?

**Mark:** Well, when we got married, we were both 36.

**Maria:** Uh-huh.

**Marion:** . . . and when we had our daughter, Tonia, we were 38. Tonia is wonderful, but it's not easy to raise a young child at our age.

**Mark:** Yeah, we're always tired!

**Maria:** I think many parents feel the same way!

**Marion:** Maybe . . . so we decided that one child is enough for us!

**Maria:** Uh-huh. And does Tonia ever feel lonely?

**Marion:** I don't think so, because we spend a lot of time with her, and she has lots of friends.

**Mark:** Yeah, she's very popular!

**Maria:** Really! You know, I heard that only children are often more popular—and more intelligent—than children with siblings.

**Mark:** Well, that's interesting!

**Maria:** Isn't it? OK, thanks! Now, let's meet Tom and Jenna Mori from New York City.

**Tom:** Hi.

**Jenna:** Hi, Maria!

**Maria:** Now, you also decided to have just one child.

**Tom:** That's right . . .

**Maria:** Tell us why.

**Tom:** Well, it was a difficult decision

**Jenna:** Uh-huh.

**Tom:** Because Jenna and I really love kids. But we're both teachers, and you know, teachers don't make a lot of money!

**Maria:** No, most teachers aren't rich!

**Jenna:** Well, we want our son Jay to have a good life—you know—a good school, piano lessons, travel . . . But today, those things are expensive!

**Maria:** I know!

**Tom:** Well, we can't pay for all those things for two children. So we decided to have only one child, because we want to give him the best of everything.

**Maria:** I understand. But does Jay ever feel lonely?

**Tom:** No, never!

**Jenna:** He's always busy with his friends and sports and his music.

**Maria:** That's wonderful! Thanks for talking with us.

**Tom and Jenna:** Our pleasure. Thank *you*!

**Maria:** OK, next, I'm going to talk to the kids! Don't go away!

#### 3C. *Listening for Details*
(repeat Section 3B)

#### 3D. *Listening between the Lines*

#### Excerpt 1

**Marion:** . . . and when we had our daughter, Tonia, we were 38. Tonia is wonderful, but it's not easy to raise a young child at our age.

**Mark:** Yeah, we're always tired!

**Maria:** I think many parents feel the same way!

**Marion:** Maybe . . . so we decided that one child is enough for us!

**Excerpt 2**

**Maria:** You know, I heard that only children are often more popular—and more intelligent—than children with siblings.

**Mark:** Well, that's interesting!

**Excerpt 3**

**Tom:** Well, we can't pay for all those things for two children. So we decided to have only one child, because we want to give him the best of everything.

## 4. LISTENING TWO: How do only kids feel?

**4A.** *Expanding the Topic*

**Maria Sanchez:** Welcome back. What do kids think about being an only child? We're going to speak to Marion and Mark's daughter, Tonia, and to Tom and Jenna's son, Jay. Hi, Tonia.

**Tonia:** Hi.

**Maria:** How old are you sweetheart?

**Tonia:** Eight.

**Maria:** Eight. And Jay, you are . . . ?

**Jay:** Thirteen.

**Maria:** OK. Now Tonia, you are the only child in your family, right?

**Tonia:** Uh-huh.

**Maria:** Do you like that?

**Tonia:** No! I hate it . . .

**Maria:** Really . . . Why?

**Tonia:** Because I want a sister.

**Maria:** Oh . . .

**Tonia:** All my friends have brothers and sisters. I'm the only kid in my class who doesn't have one!

**Maria:** Did you talk to your parents about it?

**Tonia:** Yeah. But my mom said, "I am 46 years old! I am not going to have another child."

**Maria:** And how did you feel then?

**Tonia:** I was sad.

**Maria:** But can you understand your mom and dad?

**Tonia:** Yeah.

**Maria:** Well, that's good.

**Tonia:** But I still want a sister!

**Maria:** Well, here's a little girl who knows what she wants! And Jay, do you feel the same way?

**Jay:** No, not at all. I like my family like this.

**Maria:** But do you ever feel lonely?

**Jay:** No! I feel special! I do a lot of things with my parents. We always have fun together.

**Maria:** What kinds of things do you do?

**Jay:** Well, we travel a lot. Like, this year, we're going to go skiing in Colorado.

**Maria:** That's great! But do you ever feel different from your friends?

**Jay:** No! Actually, a lot of my friends are only children too.

**Maria:** How interesting . . . Thanks Jay, and thanks to you too, Tonia.

**Tonia and Jay:** You're welcome.

**Maria:** So there you have it—two children, and two very different feelings about being an only child. Thanks for watching!

## 5. REVIEWING LANGUAGE

**5A.** *Exploring Language:* Be going to

① **Tonia:** But my mom said, "I am not *going to* have another child."

**Maria:** Today, we're gonna talk about only children.

1. Today, we are going to meet two families with only children.
2. First, we're gonna talk with Marion and Mark Gold.
3. OK, next, I'm gonna talk to the kids!
4. We're going to speak to Marion and Mark's daughter, Tonia.
5. Like, this year, we're gonna go skiing in Colorado.

## UNIT 9 ◆ THE QUIZ SHOW

## 3. LISTENING ONE: *What in the World?*

**3A.** *Introducing the Topic*

**Emily:** Hey Christina, is Mom home from work yet?

**Christina:** No, she's working late.

**Emily:** Again? She shouldn't work so much. It's time for *What in the World?*

**Christina:** I know. What channel is it on?

**Emily:** Channel 4, I think.

**Christina:** Let's watch it, OK? I'll be right there.

**Emily:** OK. It's starting. Sshhh . . .

**TV Game Show Host:** It's time to play *What in the World?*—the show where people win thousands of dollars!

**3B.** *Listening for Main Ideas*

**Emily:** Hey Christina, is Mom home from work yet?

**Christina:** No, she's working late.

**Emily:** Again? She shouldn't work so much. It's time for *What in the World?*

**Christina:** I know. What channel is it on?

**Emily:** Channel 4, I think.

**Christina:** Let's watch it, OK? I'll be right there.

**Emily:** OK. It's starting. Sshhh . . .

**TV Game Show Host:** It's time to play *What in the World?*—the show where people win thousands of dollars! Please welcome Stanley Smith, our champion. Last week Mr. Smith won $5,000. Tonight he's going to try to win more money. I'd also like to introduce our new contestant tonight, Professor Thomas Johnson. Welcome, sir.

**Professor Johnson:** Thank you. It's nice to be here.

**Emily:** Wow, a professor. He's probably really smart.

**Host:** Tonight the subject is international cuisine. Listen carefully to the question, and try to give the right answer. Good luck! Now, Mr. Smith, are you ready? Listen carefully: In Mexico this little green pepper makes the food taste spicy and hot. What is it?

**Mr. Smith:** Um, let's see . . . Is it . . . jalapeño? Yes, it's jalapeno.

**Host:** You're right! That's $1,000.

**Christina:** That was kind of hard.

**Host:** Now it's your turn, Professor Johnson. Listen carefully: People in Korea love to eat this food with almost every meal. What is it?

**Professor Johnson:** Uh, let me think. It's rice.

**Emily:** That's not fair! His question was too easy! They should ask more difficult questions!

**Host:** That's it. $1,000 for you! Now, ladies and gentlemen, here comes the big question of tonight. If our champion answers correctly, he will come back tomorrow night. If he doesn't answer correctly, he will leave the show—with $6,000. Are you ready for this one, Mr. Smith?

**Mr. Smith:** I hope so.

**Host:** Mr. Smith, many people in Asia eat their food with these. What are they?

**Mr. Smith:** Mmm, hold on. Are they—? No, that's not it. I'm not sure . . . Are they—? Ohhhh . . .

**Host:** I'm sorry, Mr. Smith. Your time is up. Now, Professor Johnson, it's your turn. If you answer this correctly, you are the new champion of *What in the World?*

**Professor Johnson:** Are they chopsticks?

**Host:** Yes! Professor Johnson, you are the new champion of *What in the World?* I'm sorry, Mr. Smith. Goodbye and good luck.

**Christina:** So the professor won. I guess he really *is* smart.

**Emily:** I don't know. It seems kind of strange to me. That chopsticks question was kind of easy. I'm surprised that Mr. Smith didn't know the answer . . .

**3C.** *Listening for Details*
(repeat Section 3B)

**3D.** *Listening between The Lines*

**Excerpt 1**

**Host:** I'd also like to introduce our new contestant tonight, Professor Thomas Johnson. Welcome, sir.

**Professor Johnson:** Thank you. It's nice to be here.

**Emily:** Wow, a professor. He's probably really smart.

**Excerpt 2**

**Host:** Tonight the subject is international cuisine. Listen carefully to the question, and try to give the right answer. Good luck! Now, Mr. Smith, are you ready? Listen carefully: In Mexico this little green pepper makes the food taste spicy and hot. What is it?

**Mr. Smith:** Um, let's see . . . Is it . . . jalapeño? Yes, it's jalapeno.

**Host:** You're right! That's $1,000.

**Christina:** That was kind of hard.

**Excerpt 3**

**Host:** Are you ready for this one, Mr. Smith?

**Mr. Smith:** I hope so.

**Host:** Mr. Smith, many people in Asia eat their food with these. What are they?

**Mr. Smith:** Mmm, hold on. Are they—? No, that's not it. I'm not sure . . . Are they—? Ohhhh . . .

**Host:** I'm sorry, Mr. Smith. Your time is up. Now,

Professor Johnson, it's your turn. If you answer this correctly, you are the new champion of *What in the World?*

**Professor Johnson:** Are they chopsticks?

**Host:** Yes! Professor Johnson, you are the new champion of *What in the World?* I'm sorry. Mr. Smith. Goodbye and good luck.

**Christina:** So the professor won. I guess he really *is* smart.

**Emily:** I don't know. It seems kind of strange to me. That chopsticks question was kind of easy. I'm surprised that Mr. Smith didn't know the answer . . .

## 4. LISTENING TWO: A Quiz Show Scandal

### 4A. *Expanding the Topic*

**News Announcer:** This is a special announcement. There's been a quiz show scandal. According to Professor Thomas Johnson—the champion of the popular TV quiz show *What in the World?*—all the contestants know the questions and answers before they play the game. Professor Johnson spoke this morning in Washington . . .

**Professor Johnson:** I am very sorry to tell you that I knew the answers. We all knew the answers. It wasn't a real game. It was just a way to make money and

make people watch the show. The TV show wanted new contestants to win because it's more exciting that way. So we gave the people what they wanted. And I was part of this . . . I wanted the money . . . I'm so very, very sorry . . .

**News Announcer:** Johnson also said today that he will not keep the $20,000 that he won on the show. He is going to give the money to a new organization called Truth in Television. This group will make sure that game shows on television are real and fair. He will give his game show money to this group, and he said that the other contestants should all do the same thing. From New York, this is Robert Sargent.

## 5. REVIEWING LANGUAGE

### 5A. *Exploring Language: Intonation*

What is jalapeño?
Where do people eat rice?
Who are the contestants?
Where do people use chopsticks?

1. What is your favorite game show?
2. When is it on television?
3. Who is the host?
4. How do the contestants win money?
5. Why are game shows fun to watch?
6. Where are game shows popular?

# ANSWER KEY

## UNIT 1 ◆
## A WORLD OF FRIENDS, A WORLD OF PEACE

### 2A. BACKGROUND
**2** a. Yes   b. I don't know   c. Yes   d. No

### 2B. VOCABULARY FOR COMPREHENSION
1. a   3. b   5. b   7. a   9. a
2. a   4. a   6. a   8. b   10. a

### 3A. INTRODUCING THE TOPIC
1. a telephone call   2. Answers will vary.

### 3B. LISTENING FOR MAIN IDEAS
**1** 1. T   2. F   3. F   4. T   5. T

**2** host families, hotels, students, sightseeing, groups, languages

### 3C. LISTENING FOR DETAILS
1. b   2. a   3. b   4. a   5. b

### 3D. LISTENING BETWEEN THE LINES
**Excerpt 1: 1.** a   **2.** a
**Excerpt 2:** a   **Excerpt 3:** c

### 4A. EXPANDING THE TOPIC
1. a   2. b   3. a   4. a   5. a   6. a

### 4B. LINKING LISTENINGS ONE AND TWO
**1** 1. Nina   5. Vadim
2. Adam/Vadim   6. Nina
3. Rick   7. Rick/Adam/Vadim
4. Adam   8. Adam/Vadim

**2** Answers will vary.

### 5A. EXPLORING LANGUAGE: Letters of the Alphabet
**2** a, e, i, o, u

### 5B. WORKING WITH WORDS
**1** *A.* **Student B's answers:**
1. b   2. b   3. a   4. b

*B.* **Student A's answers:**
1. b   2. a   3. b   4. a

**2** **Nouns:** friendship, peace, visitors
**Adjectives:** comfortable, friendly, new
**Verbs:** want, make, speak

### 6A. GRAMMAR: Present Tense of *Be*
**1** 1. **Rick:** But you know, the Friendship Force <u>isn't</u> for everyone. Some people <u>aren't</u> comfortable living with a family in a different culture for two weeks.
**Rick:** <u>What's</u> your name?
**Nina:** <u>It's</u> Nina. N-I-N-A.
2. isn't, aren't

**2** 1. 're (are)   4. aren't (are not)
2. 'm not (am not)   5. 're (are)
3. isn't (is not)

**3** 1. aren't   6. aren't
2. isn't   7. 'm
3. isn't   8. 'm not
4. 're   9. isn't
5. is

### 6B. STYLE: Telephone Talk
**1** 1. 2, 1, 3   2. 3, 1, 2

**2** Possible answers:
1. **Mrs. Marchuk:** Hello?
**Vadim:** Hi, may I please speak to Adam?
2. **Mary:** American Language Program. Mary Lee speaking.
**Ben:** Hi, I'm calling for information about your English classes.
3. **Adam:** Hello?
**Nina:** Hi, is Adam there?
**Adam:** Speaking. / This is Adam.
**Nina:** Oh, hi! This is Nina Rodriguez.

## UNIT 2 ◆
## DO YOU LIKE RAP MUSIC?

### 1B. SHARING INFORMATION
1. b
2. hip hop, hippie, hip hip a hop, bang bang boogie, scooby doo
3. Answers will vary.
4. Answers will vary.

### 2A. BACKGROUND
1. T   2. F   3. T   4. F   5. T   6. F

### 2B. VOCABULARY FOR COMPREHENSION
a. rhymes   d. popular   g. musicians
b. violence   e. rhythm   h. poor
c. famous   f. serious

### 3A. INTRODUCING THE TOPIC
1. b      2. Answers will vary.

### 3B. LISTENING FOR MAIN IDEAS
**①** 1. T      3. T      5. T      7. F
   2. T      4. F      6. T      8. F

**②** his mother, his death, his problems, his songs, his childhood

### 3C. LISTENING FOR DETAILS
**①** 1, 6, 7
**②** 2, 3, 5, 6

### 3D. LISTENING BETWEEN THE LINES
**①** **Excerpt 1:** a
   **Excerpt 2:** c
   **Excerpt 3:** c

### 4A. EXPANDING THE TOPIC
**①** a. 8      c. 6      e. 4      g. 3
   b. 2      d. 1      f. 7

### 4B. LINKING LISTENINGS ONE AND TWO
**①** Possible answers:
   1. The rapper says the words.
   2. There is no real melody.
   3. Musicians play musical instruments.
   4. Many songs are about life, problems, violence, being poor.

### 5A. EXPLORING LANGUAGE: Pronunciation of /æ/
**②** at, dance, and, began, have, fashion, rap, and, matching, hats, caps, backward, and, fashion, had, rappers

**③** 1. rap         3. caps        5. backward
   2. rappers     4. fashion     6. match

### 5B. WORKING WITH WORDS
**①** 1. instruments   4. popular   7. serious
   2. musician      5. famous    8. poor
   3. rhymes        6. rhythm    9. violence

### 6A. GRAMMAR: The Simple Past of *Be*
**①** 1. His life <u>was</u>      His family <u>was</u>
      It <u>was</u>           His songs <u>were</u>
      He <u>wasn't</u>        They <u>were</u>

   2. wasn't

**②** 1. was        7. weren't    13. were
   2. was        8. were       14. was
   3. was        9. was        15. Was
   4. was       10. wasn't     16. was
   5. were      11. was        17. wasn't
   6. Were      12. were       18. was

### 6B. STYLE: Asking for and Giving Definitions and Explanations
Possible answers:
*A.*
**Student B:**
1. What is *graffiti*?
2. What is *break dancing*?
3. What is a *rapper*?
4. What does *rhyme* mean?

*B.*
**Student A:**
1. What is a *DJ*?
2. What does *nonsense* mean?
3. What is *gangsta rap*?
4. What are *drum machines*?

## UNIT 3 ◆ DIAMONDS ARE FOREVER

### 2A. BACKGROUND
1. People first wore diamond engagement rings in the 1600s in Europe.
2. In the 1800s, people found diamonds in South Africa.
3. Cecil Rhodes started the De Beers Group in South Africa.
4. Cecil Rhodes started the De Beers Group in the late 1800s.
5. The two countries were the United States and Japan.

### 2B. VOCABULARY FOR COMPREHENSION
1. a      3. a      5. b      7. a      9. a
2. a      4. a      6. a      8. b

### 3A. INTRODUCING THE TOPIC
1. I don't know.      2. Yes      3. No

### 3B. LISTENING FOR MAIN IDEAS
1. King Louis XIV of France bought the Hope Diamond.
2. Henry Philip Hope bought the Hope Diamond.
3. A wealthy woman bought the diamond and she had bad luck.

### 3C. LISTENING FOR DETAILS
1. b      2. b      3. a      4. b      5. a      6. a

### 3D. LISTENING BETWEEN THE LINES
**Excerpt 1:** b      **Excerpt 2:** b      **Excerpt 3:** b

### 4A. EXPANDING THE TOPIC
**①** cut      color      clarity      carat
      2         1           4            3

**②** 1. T      2. T      3. F      4. F

### 4B. LINKING LISTENINGS ONE AND TWO
Possible answers:
1. color, cut, carat      2. color, carat

## 5A. EXPLORING LANGUAGE: Rising Intonation

**2** **Student B answers:**
1. Yes, I do.
2. No, it has three pearls.
3. No, they aren't.
4. Yes, I do.
5. Answers will vary.
6. Answers will vary.

**Student A answers:**
1. Yes, I do.
2. No, it has five pearls.
3. No, they are large.
4. Yes, I do.
5. Answers will vary.
6. Answers will vary.

## 5B. WORKING WITH WORDS

1. valuable
2. huge
3. carats
4. sparkles
5. fascinating
6. stole
7. wealthy

## 6A. GRAMMAR: The Simple Present

**1**
a. sparkles; weighs
b. Sentences 4 (doesn't mean) and 5 (don't cost) are negative.
c. Sentence 7 is a yes/no question.

**2**
1. ask
2. see
3. read
4. don't know
5. use
6. becomes
7. wears
8. opens
9. wears
10. isn't
11. Do you see
12. weighs
13. sparkles
14. comes
15. wear
16. sounds
17. brings
18. have

## 6B. STYLE: Making Suggestions

**1** 1. a    2. a    3. b

**2** Possible answers:
B: Let's go
A: How about going / Why don't we go

## 7A. SPEAKING TOPICS: Proverbs or Sayings

**1** 1. c    2. d    3. a    4. b

# UNIT 4 ◆ MEMORIES: LOST AND FOUND

## 2A. BACKGROUND

**2** a. 6    b. 5    c. 8    d. 2, 4

## 2B. VOCABULARY FOR COMPREHENSION

1. a    3. a    5. b    7. a
2. a    4. a    6. b    8. a

## 3A. INTRODUCING THE TOPIC

Answers will vary.

## 3B. LISTENING FOR MAIN IDEAS

**1** 1. T  2. T  3. T  4. F  5. T  6. F  7. T

**2** writing stories, making friends, feeling lonely, childhood memories, remembering names, support groups

## 3C. LISTENING FOR DETAILS

1. a    2. b    3. c    4. a    5. c    6. b

## 3D. LISTENING BETWEEN THE LINES

**1** **Excerpt 1:** b    **Excerpt 2:** b    **Excerpt 3:** a

## 4A. EXPANDING THE TOPIC

**1** 1. T    2. T    3. T    4. F    5. T    6. F

## 4B. LINKING LISTENINGS ONE AND TWO

**1** Possible answers:

| People with Alzheimer's have lost: | People in the writers' group have found: |
|---|---|
| their memories | new friends |
| their friends | a new hobby |
| their jobs | support |
| their hobbies | happiness, pleasure |
| their independence | people who understand them |

## 5A. EXPLORING LANGUAGE: Pronunciation of /ey/ and /ɛ/

**2**
1. /ɛ/    3. /ey/    5. /ey/    7. /ey/
2. /ɛ/    4. /ɛ/    6. /ɛ/    8. /ɛ/

**3**
1. Well /ɛ/, say /ey/
2. came /ey/, famous /ey/, named /ey/
3. met /ɛ/
4. remember /ɛ/
5. forgetting /ɛ/, every /ɛ/, day /ey/
6. way /ey/, help /ɛ/
7. day /ey/
8. great /ey/
9. together /ɛ/

## 5B. WORKING WITH WORDS

**1** **Student B's answers:**
1. b
2. a
3. d
4. c

**Student A's answers:**
5. f
6. h
7. e
8. g

1. S  2. S  3. D  4. D  5. S  6. D  7. S

## 6A. GRAMMAR: Subject and Object Pronouns

**1** a. I, she    b. me, her

**2**
1. It
2. you
3. I
4. He
5. they
6. them
7. us
8. I
9. her
10. She
11. I
12. it
13. him

6B. STYLE: Expressing Interest in a Conversation

Answers will vary.

## UNIT 5 ◆
## THINKING YOUNG: CREATIVITY IN BUSINESS

### 2A. BACKGROUND

**②** 1. a    2. b    3. b

### 2B. VOCABULARY FOR COMPREHENSION

**①** 1. a    3. b    5. a    7. a    9. a
2. b    4. b    6. b    8. b    10. a

**②** 1. e    3. f    5. d    7. i    9. b
2. a    4. j    6. h    8. c    10. g

### 3A. INTRODUCING THE TOPIC

1. a    2. b    3. a

### 3B. LISTENING FOR MAIN IDEAS

1. F
2. F    K-K made the first pair of Wristies by herself.
3. T
4. T
5. F    K-K and her mother were not afraid to start a business.
6. T

### 3C. LISTENING FOR DETAILS

1. c    2. a    3. b    4. c    5. a

### 3D. LISTENING BETWEEN THE LINES

**Excerpt 1:** b    **Excerpt 2:** c    **Excerpt 3:** b

### 4A. EXPANDING THE TOPIC

**①** 1. F    2. T    3. T    4. T    5. F    6. T

### 4B. LINKING LISTENINGS ONE AND TWO

**①** 1. K-K Gregory       5. K-K's mother
2. student          6. Professor Ray
3. Professor Ray    7. K-K's mother
4. K-K Gregory

### 5A. EXPLORING LANGUAGE:
Pronunciation of "th"

**②** 1. They're, with       5. mother, anything
2. There's, the, thumb   6. them, there's
3. them, others, them
4. then, thought, these, things

**③** 1. thinks      3. anything    5. thumb
2. mother      4. thought

### 5B. WORKING WITH WORDS

**①** 1. advice     4. owner       6. exciting
2. afraid     5. successful  7. experience
3. creative

### 6A. GRAMMAR: *There is/There are, There was/There were*

**①** 1. Yeah, <u>there were</u> problems! For example, business was very slow at first because <u>there weren't</u> any other people in my company. <u>There was</u> only one person—me! Now <u>there are</u> three employees.
2. Present: there are
Past: there were, there was, there weren't
3. <u>Are there</u> any more questions?
Yes. <u>Were there</u> any problems in the beginning?
4. any

**②** 1. there aren't   5. There are    9. There were
2. There was     6. there are    10. there are
3. there aren't  7. there isn't  11. There is
4. Was there     8. There is

### 6B. STYLE: Explaining How to Do Something

**①** Possible answers:
1. This is how      4. Next / Then
2. First            5. Finally
3. Then / Next      6. And that's how

## UNIT 6 ◆
## FROM SADNESS TO STRENGTH

### 1B. SHARING INFORMATION

**①** 1. c    2. d    3. a    4. f    5. b    6. e

**②** 1. Margaret Thatcher, Hillary Clinton
2. Indira Gandhi (daughter of Jawaharlal Nehru, the first prime minister of India from 1947 to 1964), Hillary Clinton (wife of Bill Clinton, president of the United States from 1993 to 2001, Eva Peron (wife of Juan Peron, president of Argentina from 1946 to 1955)
3. Answers will vary.

### 2A. BACKGROUND

1. b    2. a    3. b    4. b

### 2B. VOCABULARY FOR COMPREHENSION

1. a traditional   4. speeches    7. popular
2. independent     5. speak out   8. first lady
3. politics        6. respected   9. political

## 3B. LISTENING FOR MAIN IDEAS

**1** 1. F    2. F    3. F    4. T    5. T    6. F

**2** 2, 3, 5, 6, 7, 8

## 3C. LISTENING FOR DETAILS

1. b    2. a    3. b    4. a    5. b    6. b    7. a

## 3D. LISTENING BETWEEN THE LINES

**Excerpt 1:** a    **Excerpt 2:** b    **Excerpt 3:** a

## 4A. EXPANDING THE TOPIC

**1** 1. T    2. F    3. T    4. F    5. T    6. F

## 4B. LINKING LISTENINGS ONE AND TWO

**1** 1. Before    3. Before    5. After
2. After    4. After

## 5A. EXPLORING LANGUAGE:
### Pronunciation of -ed endings

**1** 1. /t/    3. /d/    5. /d/    7. /ɪd/    9. /ɪd/
2. /d/    4. /t/    6. /t/    8. /d/

**2** 1. /t/, /d/    4. /d/, /t/    7. /ɪd/, /d/
2. /ɪd/    5. /ɪd/    8. /d/, /ɪd/
3. /ɪd/    6. /d/, /d/

## 5B. WORKING WITH WORDS

**1** 1. political    3. strong    5. speech
2. poor    4. speak out    6. respected

## 6A. GRAMMAR: Simple Past Tense

**1** 1. a. died    2. a. became
    b. started        b. wrote
    c. worked        c. said
    d. helped        d. lost
    e. loved
    f. tried
    g. learned
    h. died
3. She <u>didn't stop</u> working for women, children, and poor people.
4. After FDR died, <u>what did Eleanor Roosevelt do</u>?

**2** 1. was not/wasn't    12. said
2. studied    13. spoke
3. copied    14. had
4. wanted    15. turned
5. were    16. decided
6. had    17. did not stop/
7. worked        didn't stop
8. moved    18. became
9. worked    19. lived
10. did not like/    20. did . . . live
    didn't like    21. Did . . . write
11. did not agree/
    didn't agree

## 6B. STYLE: Asking for Examples

**Student A's answers:**    **Student B's answers.**
1. b    4. f
2. a    5. e
3. c    6. d

# UNIT 7 ◆
# DRIVING YOU CRAZY

## 1B. SHARING INFORMATION

1. C    2. A    3. B

## 2A. BACKGROUND

1. 4    3. riding a bicycle
2. 335    4. 50

## 2B. VOCABULARY FOR COMPREHENSION

1. a    2. b    3. a    4. a    5. b    6. a    7. a    8. a

## 3A. INTRODUCING THE TOPIC

1. Road rage means getting angry at other drivers.
2. Road rage is dangerous because people can be injured or killed.
3. Answers will vary.

## 3B. LISTENING FOR MAIN IDEAS

John: 2, 3, 5
Marie: 1, 3, 4, 6

## 3C. LISTENING FOR DETAILS

1. T    3. T    5. F    7. T    9. F
2. T    4. F    6. T    8. F    10. F

## 3D. LISTENING BETWEEN THE LINES

**Excerpt 1:**    **Excerpt 2:**
1. John felt scared.    1. Marie felt angry.
2. He feels lucky.    2. Marie feels angry now.
3. Yes, he's probably a good driver.    3. Marie is usually a polite driver.
4. The truck driver felt angry.

**Excerpt 3:**
1. Stress causes road rage.
2. The teacher wants his students to feel less stressed.
3. Yes, he is probably a good teacher because he is teaching his students how to control their own road rage.

## 4A. EXPANDING THE TOPIC

1. b    2. b    3. b    4. a    5. b

## 4B. LINKING LISTENINGS ONE AND TWO

Possible answers:
1. The truck driver probably feels angry. He will probably start honking his horn. He may scare the slow driver.

2. Allen probably feels very scared. He may slow down or change lanes to avoid the angry truck driver.
3. Answers will vary.

## 5A. EXPLORING LANGUAGE: Syllables

**1** 1. <u>rage</u> (1)        4. a·<u>non</u>·y·mous (4)
   2. <u>an</u>·gry (2)      5. <u>pho</u>·bi·a (3)
   3. <u>sto</u>·ry (2)      6. in·ter·<u>sec</u>·tion (4)

**2** **Student B's answers:**    **Student A's answers:**
   1. 1                    6. 1
   2. 2                    7. 3
   3. 3                    8. 2
   4. 2                    9. 2
   5. 3                    10. 3

## 5B. WORKING WITH WORDS

**1** 1. crowded         4. control
   2. stressed out     5. rude
   3. get injured      6. anonymous

**2** Answers will vary.

## 6A. GRAMMAR: Comparative Adjectives

**1** 1. The adjective is *faster*. It ends with *-er*.
   2. The adjective is *polite*. The word that comes before it is *more*.
   3. The word that comes after the adjective in both sentences is *than*.

**2** 1. more crowded, safer    4. longer
   2. angrier                5. worse
   3. faster                 6. more comfortable

**3** Answers will vary. The comparative adjectives are *newer, longer, shorter, more colorful, older* and *taller*.

## 6B. STYLE: Expressing Similar Feelings and Experiences

Answers will vary.

## UNIT 8 ◆
## ONLY CHILD—LONELY CHILD

### 2A. BACKGROUND

1. The number of only children in the United States is going up.
2. In New York City, many more families have only children than in the rest of the United States.

### 2B. VOCABULARY FOR COMPREHENSION

1. got married      5. busy
2. had a child      6. spend time with
3. tired            7. sibling
4. raise            8. expensive

## 3A. INTRODUCING THE TOPIC

1. a      2. a        3. Answers will vary.

## 3B. LISTENING FOR MAIN IDEAS

1. more        4. lonely       6. a good life
2. difficult   5. money        7. busy
3. old

## 3C. LISTENING FOR DETAILS

1. T  2. T  3. T  4. T  5. F  6. T  7. T  8. F

## 3D. LISTENING BETWEEN THE LINES

**Excerpt 1:** a      **Excerpt 2:** a      **Excerpt 3:** b

## 4A. EXPANDING THE TOPIC

1. c  2. a  3. b  4. b  5. c  6. b  7. a  8. b

## 4B. LINKING LISTENINGS ONE AND TWO

**1** Answers will vary.

**2** Possible reasons from Listenings One and Two:
   2. The parents don't have enough money.
   3. The parents are too tired or too busy with their jobs.

## 5A. EXPLORING LANGUAGE: *Be going to*

**1** 1. a    2. b    3. b    4. a    5. b

**2** Answers will vary.

## 5B. WORKING WITH WORDS

**Student B's answers:**      **Student A's answers:**
1. raise                     5. have
2. busy                      6. got married
3. tired                     7. decide
4. spent . . . time          8. kid
                             9. sibling
                             10. only children

## 6A. GRAMMAR: The Future with *Be going to*

**1** 1. 3 parts
   2. *be*
   3. *going to.* No, it doesn't change.
   4. the base form of the verb

**2** 1. Are you going to
   2. I am (I'm) going to
   3. are not (aren't) going to
   4. They are (They're) going to
   6. I am (I'm) going to, I am (I'm) going to
   7. are ('re) going to be

## 6B STYLE: Explaining Reasons with *Because*

**1** 1. c    2. a    3. b

**2** 1. c    2. a    3. b    4. e    5. d

**3** Answers will vary.

## UNIT 9 ◆
## THE QUIZ SHOW

### 2A. BACKGROUND

1. They had to answer difficult questions to win money.
2. They were unhappy when they found out that some of the quiz shows were not real games. They were not real games because some players got the answers to the questions before the show.
3. Answers will vary.

### 2B. VOCABULARY FOR COMPREHENSION

| | | | | |
|---|---|---|---|---|
| 1. d | 3. i | 5. h | 7. f | 9. g |
| 2. e | 4. a | 6. b | 8. j | 10. c |

### 3A. INTRODUCING THE TOPIC

1. a game show
2. Possible answers: music, questions, names of winners

### 3B. LISTENING FOR MAIN IDEAS

**1** 1. b    2. b    3. c    4. a    5. a    6. c

### 3C. LISTENING FOR DETAILS

| | | | |
|---|---|---|---|
| 1. True | 3. False | 5. False | 7. True |
| 2. True | 4. False | 6. False | 8. True |

### 3D. LISTENING BETWEEN THE LINES

**Excerpt 1:** a
**Excerpt 2:** b
**Excerpt 3:** 1. b    2. a    3. b

### 4A. EXPANDING THE TOPIC

**1** Possible answers:
1. A quiz show scandal is when people think something is bad or wrong with a quiz show.
2. He is going to talk about the quiz show scandal.
3. He probably feels guilty, nervous, or scared.

**2** 1, 4

**3** Answers will vary.

**4** Answers will vary.

### 4B. LINKING LISTENINGS ONE AND TWO

Possible answers:
1. People wanted Professor Johnson to win because they thought he was smart.
2. Christina and Emily will feel surprised and angry because they thought the quiz show was real.
3. Other players will feel surprised and angry because Professor Johnson did not win fairly.

### 5B. WORKING WITH WORDS

Answers will vary.

### 6A. GRAMMAR: *Should*

**1** a, c

**2** In the first sentence, *should* means advice. In the second sentence, *should* means something that is a good thing to do.

**3**
| | | |
|---|---|---|
| 1. should | 4. should | 7. Should |
| 2. should | 5. shouldn't | 8. should |
| 3. shouldn't | 6. should | |

Credits

Page 20, *Rapper's Delight*, by Bernard Edwards, Nile Rodgers. © 1979 Bernard's Other Music (CMI) & Sony Songs, Inc. (BMI). All Rights o/b/o Bernard's Other Music (BMI). Administered by Warner-Tamerlane Publishing Corp. (BMI). All Rights Reserved. Used by Permission. Warner Bros. Publications U.S. Inc., Miami, Florida 33014.

Page 26, *Keep Ya Head Up*, by Tupac Shakur D. Anderson and Roger Troutman. © 1993 Warner-Tamerlane Publishing Corp., Ghetto Gospel Music, Inc. Interscope Pearl Music, Inc. All rights o/b/o Ghetto Gospel Music, Inc. and Interscope Pearl Music, Inc. Administered by Warner-Tamerlane Publishing Corp. All Rights for Rubber Band Music, Inc. administered by Songs of Polygram International Inc. All Rights Reserved. Used by Permission. Warner Bros. Publications U.S. Inc., Miami, Florida 33014.